Mental

Models

A Step by Step Guide to Improving
Your Critical Thinking

*(A Collection of Thinking Tools Helping You to
Manage Productivity)*

Esther Humble

Published By **Oliver Leish**

Esther Humble

Mental Models: A Step by Step Guide to Improving Your Critical Thinking (A Collection of Thinking Tools Helping You to Manage Productivity)

ISBN 978-1-77485-694-9

Legal & Disclaimer

Table Of Contents

Chapter 1: What The Mental Models?

It's not uncommon to get stuck in your thinking. If it's about workplace issue, a disagreement with someone else or even a issue that you've noticed in yourself at one point or another our minds may seem like we've hit an impasse. Our perceptions are limited to the vastness that is the universe and the situations surrounding us. If you've ever been caught within a rut of unproductive thinking, then you'll need fresh mental frameworks.

Mental models as camera lenses

Are they mental models? They are basically perspectives. Imagine a camera that is fancy that has lens that are removable. Imagine yourself on the beach looking forward to the sunset. To get the most beautiful picture possible, you switch out several lenses in order to capture various aspects of the scene. When the sun is gone while the sky's brimming with stars, certain lenses won't work as well in the night and you switch to different lenses.

Although you don't control what's happening in the real world however, your mental models can provide various perspectives. In most situations, some models are more effective than other models. For instance using scientific methods is generally the norm for research, but it might not be the best choice in other situations, such as solving a personal issue with a companion. Understanding that certain mental models can be limiting is as crucial as utilizing new ones. If you're cognizant of what mental structures that you rely on, you will be able to learn more about the reasons you behave and think how you do.

Mental models allow you to see the world in different and intriguing ways. You'll see various aspects and broaden your knowledge. If you were to rely on just one model for navigating through the universe is overwhelming and ineffective having a variety of models will make your life simpler. You'll have a broader and more precise understanding of the issues in front of you, regardless of whether it's a dilemma, decision or concept.

How do we build mental models?

Mental models are just as old as humankind itself. Animals too have mental models, even though they are mostly basic and rely on the basic instincts about things like food. For instance the rat that is trapped who is in a maze understands that if he completes the maze, he will receive rewards. The entire way of thinking revolves on the assumption that running equals treats. For humans, every person has at some point a mental model they use. You're more likely to have several however you might not even know about them.

The mental models we construct are in response to how we were taught as children and on what we've been taught in light of our experiences. If you don't have a deeper to your perspective then it will never expand. In order to reach the highest levels of understanding and thinking individuals must deliberately and actively accept diverse mental models. Charlie Munger is a great example of someone who is consciously thinking.

Charlie Munger, Vice Chairman of the giant holding firm Berkshire Hathaway, has always been fascinated by mental models. He has also introduced the finance and business world to the idea. In his speeches, Munger describes how his worldview is based on an "latticework" made up of models in his mind. He is particularly attracted to problem-solving, however the concept of a tapestry made of mental models could be applied to other fields as well. Munger believes that the greater number of mental models you can use you'll be more mobile and flexible you'll be. The sensation of feeling "stuck" isn't frequently when faced with challenges.

Mental models can be beneficial.

Mental models are located in the fields of philosophy, science and business, as well as religion and other locations. The notion that you require multiple mental models is an example of a mental model. What is the point of learning about models and experimenting with them? They can assist you in expanding your knowledge and comprehension But what are the most tangible advantages? There are a variety of benefits:

More imagination

There are many mental models that you'll never get rid of them. This book we'll go over a lot of them of them, but there are many more. Whatever decision or problem you're confronted with, whether it's at working or in your personal life, there's an alternative mental model that you can utilize to take the opposite approach. The process of examining mental models can increase your mental capacity and challenge your brain which leads to more energy and inspiration. It's less likely that you'll feel stuck or as if you've hit a brick wall in the event that you have a second mental model to play with.

Aid in making decisions

There are many mental models that are specifically designed to aid in decision-making by removing options. Most people struggle to make a choice because there are so many options and their emotions can get in the way however, with mental models, it is possible to concentrate and follow the steps to identify the best option. Utilizing mental models to help make decisions is so valuable and we've got an entire chapter dedicated to it.

Better time management

Many people struggle managing their time For some people, it can be painful. Our thoughts can spiral out of control, forming chaos and be unorganized, and nothing can get accomplished. A good mental model can help you focus only on one particular thing at a given time, help you break down huge quantities of information or complicated scenarios, and set your priorities.

This can be used in any circumstance.

You'll see a variety of blogs and articles about using mental models in workplace situations However, the reality is that the majority of mental models serve multiple functions. They can be used in the workplace and in your private life, including family issues, relationship problems and self-reflection. You'll gain greater clarity and understanding in each aspect within your daily life.

Let you reconsider what is important to you.

Many mental models are designed for making decisions about the priorities and narrowing your scope. Instead of being overwhelmed by multiple choices and choices or trying to avoid an issue because it's too difficult to comprehend, models can help to sort through the chaos. If it's getting rid of the most unhelpful options during the course of a brainstorming session at work or dealing with anxiety about social situations Many mental models can assist you in getting down to the heart of the issue you're facing. You'll be less overwhelmed and confused, and will feel more confident in your thoughts and life. With this clarity, you'll be able to see the most important things.

Change your habits

The most significant advantage of creating mental models is the fact that it will alter your behavior. By using mental models you are able to adapt to any circumstance and look at it in a fresh way. It is possible to streamline your working style, put off work less or prioritize tasks in a manner that increases happiness. You may even be more compassionate and understanding with other people.

Mental models for all aspects of your life

In the coming 5 chapters we'll explore mental models for each aspect that you live. A variety of models can be beneficial in multiple areas and we'll make certain to mention that. The life aspects that we'll cover are making decisions taking decisions, seeing things with greater clarity and problem-solving, dealing with relationships, and encouraging positive thinking.

Chapter 2: Understanding How Our Mind How It Works

The mind that makes about our thoughts is an amazing place. But, if it is what is its distinction in the cerebral cortex? Do you believe there is in fact an underlying spirit that coordinates our thoughts or do they think they are completely resolved through the results of our scientific knowledge? Is that mouse rushing through your yard be thinking of deep thoughts, or are individuals truly individual?

In the past, before there existed subjective science prior to the time there was neurobiology, before there was any science at all, humanists have wrestled with these questions. In general, reasoning of the minds researchers from the West have been either way or the other side of the brain/body debate.

Dualists believe that the brain functions the same way regardless of regardless of whether it's an actual body. Dualists believe that there's something special about the mind - it's more than an amazing and fascinating machine. Tables, trees and billiard balls could be defined by the material sciences and science, but you must include the bonus of a non-physical characteristic, in order to understand the human mind.

On the other side are physicalists. The majority of savants today have found the physicalist argument all more convincing, namely that mental wonders are based on either a neurophysiological or physiological basis. In reality, that simple declaration, however, brings many questions. As an example, in the event that the term "physicalism" is described as all physical then what exactly is "physical" means? Physical scientists aren't likely to look at seats as often, yet seats are composed of all the materials that material science studies like particles and Atoms.

Functionalists claim they believe that the brain is what that the cerebrum is and that is a process view. There are many views in a variety of physical media. A person with a completely exclusive science might even be able to limit themselves to thinking. Character scholars, in turn emphasize that the brain is the psyche and it's as straightforward as it gets.

The Mind that is Unconscious

The remainder of your work is your inscrutable personality. It's hard to reach since you're not conscious of the things that happen the midst, but trust me when I say:

Your inscrutable personality is remarkable.

It is responsible for a lot of the functions of your body, such as breathing and processing, dozing temperature control, pulse and more - all without touching your fingers (and it also controls temperature too).

It ensures that you are trying to stay in line with the norm this is why that you may are uncomfortable when trying to introduce a new feature. Your mind must guide you back to what's recognized and thus'safe'.

*It's your seat for your emotions.

It's where your imagination and creativity come from.

It's also where your propensities are developed and maintained I'll come back to that later.

Your subliminal personality follows the rules from your conscious personality.

It causes you to react when you are weakened by something - your strength is weakened or strengthened or when your battle or flight reaction begins to kick in.

*It stores and retrieves long-term memories.

The cerebrum is the brain functions as a PC. It creates data it receives from the body's faculties and the brain and then relays the information towards the brain. Whatever the case it is true that the mind does much more than machines is able to: humans are able to think and feel emotions with their cerebrums. It is the basis of human wisdom.

The human cerebrum is typically about the size of two hands, and weighs around 1.5 kilograms. On the outside, it appears something like a pecan-like structure with its folds and fissures. Mind tissue is made up of approximately 100 billion neuron cells (neurons) and one trillion support cells that help to stabilize the tissue.

There are several parts of mind that each have its individual capacities:

*The cerebrum

*The diencephalon which includes the thalamus pituitary, nerve center, and pituitary organ

*The mind stem, including the midbrain, pons , and the medulla

*The cerebellum

What is the reason why it important to know the way your brain works?

Finally this knowledge gives you more control in utilizing the collective power of your oblivious and cognizant minds and think in an solid, flexible, adaptable and objective manner.

The advantages include improved self-esteem as well as less-energetic change , and a more evident ability to achieve the things you require in everyday life.

*THE Role of MENTAL MODELS

The significance of mental model graphs is complicated. One of the most powerful options is use it to create an annual plan for ten years to understand the state of your company and where you're headingand where it is likely to take a direct route. The majority of businesses are focused on the things they have to do in the near long term, but are not necessarily focused on the long future. Mental models can be a glimpse at the long-term, drawing out the different areas. Imagine there's an opening underneath some of the towers, and you're required to assist this area, or maybe there's a tower that isn't strengthened and you want to provide more assistance, at this point, the map acts as a guide to see the holes that exist. At this point, you'll draw them out and declare, "OK, we're going be able to understand this in 2009 and then we'll be able to look into it in the year 2010."

It's also a new aspect to this: a lot of people in organizations nowadays are aware that clients should be the ones to start with the basics. It's a universal principle however they have significant difficulties in understanding the mind of the client. Therefore, you ask them the question, "How is this going to help your client?" They respond in regards to the things they will be doing. However, it there is no certain match. The intensity of the upper section of the graph can be seen in the language are used to describe the different towers as well as the numerous boxes within the towers. Each of these words begin by using action terms. I believe that action words improve the peruser's planner's or business administrator's knowledge of what's happening inside the mind of the individual. It's a fantastic way to gain access into the mind of someone else.

Mental models are incredibly infused with assumptions or theories that affect our perception of the world and the way we decide to decision. The various terms we employ to describe mental models include viewpoints beliefs, convictions, suppositions and outlook, just to name several examples. Mental models are usually the most effective barriers to the execution of new ideas in associations but they are also the realm of hierarchical understanding where associations can be of the most significant impact.

Unfortunately often used to refer towards mental representations, carry negative connotations for the majority of us. We've all heard that familiar phrase "You know the consequences of accepting believe in it? It creates a _____ out of me and you." You can fill the blanks. Suggestions, however are the most fundamental way to understand our mind-boggling world. It's absurd to think that we are able to be able to provide complete data on every circumstance that we experience and, therefore, by their nature, our assumptions or mental models aren't perfect and therefore insufficient. In general, however our mental models perform effectively for us.

There are instances in which our mental models steer us off course. A stunning example of how flawed mental models are can stem from the old tale of visually impaired people and the elephant. some visually impaired people feel various parts of an elephant and illustrating the elephant. The representations without the input of anyone else's input are not accurate, however when combined gives a clearer but still flawed representation of what an elephant looks like. Mental models are like astounding pieces that need to put together to form a larger whole. When various mental models are observed as they are, another piece is thrown in the right place, and we get the picture more clearly but in this case we don't possess the highest level of the riddle to guide our thoughts. We must follow the same path as the visually impaired people.

Mental models affect what we see in our surroundings and provide instances of behavior. In the model presented at the beginning of the article employee perceives an overbearing, controlling chief and the administrator is able to see people who have to be placed on the base. As a result, the workers are dispersed, and the director is attempting to control more of them which is not a good thing for any company. The more the director tries to control the situation is the more dispersed workers are, which brings about a destructive cycle. The main part in the process, the actions can strengthen the invisible part, the beliefs and mental model.

What skills do people require to develop?

So how do you get out of this kind of winding that is descending? The first step is to recognize the gap between what we consider as valid and what's evident or, to put it more clearly, the gap between mental models and realities. There are two basic areas of skills that people are able to work with mental models: 1)) abilities to reflect and 2)) capabilities of asking.

Reflection abilities can hinder our thinking with the intention to be more aware of the ways we build our mental model and the way they affect our actions. This can be done in various ways. One option is to to be increasingly aware of what we are observing the moment we engage in what is often described being "jumps of deliberation" which means mentioning assumptions based on our actual facts, but without evidence to support it. In the model of an administrator it is the representative who observes the supervisor, asking for a sense however, he or she doesn't follow through on the suggestion. The employee at this point is able to conclude that the trough really does not care about the thoughts of subordinates. So, the director is watching the departure and concludes that it's due to the basis that representatives aren't thinking about their job. One method to keep an appropriate separation from this conflict is to ask:

*"What do I base my information on which my conclusions or theories are upon?"

*"Have I ever had any evidence to disprove the validity of my assertions?"

*"Am I prepared to consider how possible the possibility is beliefs could be wrong?"

Another approach to build up the capacity of reflection is often referred to as finding"left hand segment. "left-hand section." This "left-hand section" refers to the thoughts which we often have in conversations, but they aren't articulate. When we record these ideas in the future and making our mental models visible. For example, an person who sees his staff as impartial could organize an assembly of experts in his field of expertise to decide on a important direction for his team. After displaying the thought, he demands responses and receives silence. His quick idea might be, "Man! What's it going to require to start an ember under these people?" If an employee responds with only a little help or apathy, he could also be thinking, "Goodness wow! We'll try the lip management again! Shouldn't they possess an independent mind?" Each of these responses strengthens his psychological framework however, merely thinking about them allows him to free himself from the belief system to begin to look at the facts about it, or a speculation.

The final method to develop capacities for reflecting is to be able to discern the gap between what declare we believe and our belief system, and the actual actions we take and how our hypothesis is being applied. In other words it is time to begin contrasting our actions with our words or actions. Utilizing the model of an administrator representative again, the manager could be willing to admit that participative basic leadership creates a positive group, but his behavior doesn't convey the right message to his employees. If he doesn't recognize the hole there is no way to change or learn. will occur.

How we handle requests determines how we respond to requests in intimate and personal communication. After we've started to practice our skills of reflection, we'll then be able to discuss your psychological theories with other people. While doing this we must remember how our models of psychological functioning are only parts of the puzzle. In his book, The skilled Facilitator, Roger Schwarz has developed a method he calls the common model of learning that will help people improve their interpersonal skills. It is based on the belief that all people see things in a unique wayand it's these distinctions that open possibilities for creativity and learning. It's also based by the belief that everyone acts with integrity. You can practice the standard learning model using:

Test your assumptions by articulating them, and then requesting confirmation or denial;

Sharing all relevant information: retaining data may result in a less accurate picture.

Be honest by putting your ideas on the table , as opposed to your finalized concept;

Focusing on interests, not positions, which means discussing and acquiescing to the results prior to jumping to arrangements;

Discussion of those thoughts within your "left-hand segment" which are often driving your actions;

Promotions that are balanced with requests which is, requesting more information on various perspectives, as long as you can clarify your personal perspective.

These skills, when combined with the abilities to reflect, give us the capacity to alter mental models and begin making the group more changes that are practical. To change our behavior, we must first modify the beliefs upon which our actions are founded.

How can companies be able to shift mental models from blockage into use?

Mental models are the most difficult place to create an learning relationship, however it could provide the most accurate measure of the progress made. Making and shaping mental models requires altering both the individual and the authoritative behavior. It is a daunting task, in the ideal scenario. It's a process that requires patience and perseverance. The following conditions can assist associations in removing the obstacles to surfacing and examining mental models:

Create a safe space where employees feel comfortable in surfacing and reviewing their mental models. It must also be a place that decisions are based in the best interests of your company rather than on legal issues;

• Help your employees build their ability to reflect and ask for help;

*Promote a variety of varieties as opposed to congruity

You can agree to disagree; everyone isn't required to be a part of the many mental models; each one is just an additional fragment of data.

Be comfortable with your vulnerability, we'll never get the whole story.

This process requires individuals and organizations to alter their perception of the notion of work. Once those obstacles are eliminated the group can begin to realize that mental models are influences that are a focus for development. These negative strengthening circles transform to upward spirals of success.

Chapter 3: How You Can Enhance The Ability To Make Decisions

If you're faced with the need to make a decision What is your preferred way to take the decision? Do you decide immediately and then follow up or would you postpone your decision to a later time?

Many experts suggest that a quick decision is based on different opinions however, it may also lead to mistakes. Additionally, some choices can be irreversible, even if they aren't leading to negative outcomes. A reliable method should be a part of the most out of your choice.

Certainly, important decisions arise from a thorough understanding of the scenario. If you don't fully comprehend or you have an abundance of risk in your brain. However, knowing the data can allow you to enhance the outcome of your choice.

What is the strategy that works? It's simple. Use the methods below.

The most efficient method to improve your decision making skills is to increase your level of skill.

Stage 1. Review the advantages and the repercussions of your decision

Find a piece of paper, draw two-sections, then write 'Favorable circumstances' on the left section and at the right section obstacles.' Write down all of the advantages and disadvantages that you might consider in the decision you make.

Stage 2. Review your list of positive conditions and negative

Assess each preferred location or detriment that you've documented with a scale of 10 points that goes from insignificant to major. If the preferred place or burden is insignificant or not important, you can give it a rating of "1", but only you must be sure that it's significant in terms of its leeway or drawback, you can estimate it to at a maximum of 10 points. It's neither relevant nor significant. Your rate will be within the limits.

Stage 3. Incorporate all of the goals

Take the focus you provided for every bit of flexibility or disadvantage of your choice. From the total number of centers, it will be able to determine which is more extensive in terms of centers in comparison to the other.

You can choose to go with the one with the distinctive amount of centers.

If the focus is pretty close, you could try the method again, without making reference to the prior one. This is known as an 'episode. It can be repeated several times to confirm your choice.

Making Your Choice

After applying the methods above and coming to a point where the strengths are greater than the weak points, evaluate your decision by answering the related questions.

1. Does your choice have to be sincerely based?

Do you really need to make a decision? Should you not be, this moment, it's better to allow yourself more time to think about your decision. Risks are lessened with time. Longer duration can give more chances to address problems.

2. Is your decision extraordinary?

What are the most extraordinary decisions you have made? Making the decision to get married or changing your lifestyle are examples. It is a long-term commitment or reneging on a similar arrangement, so you must be mindful of the consequences of your decision.

3. Is your personality influenced by your choice?

If the person with the most identity is influenced by the choice is yours then your choice should be quick. If you make a decision that goes wrong there's no one to judge you at this point. If your decision has an impact on others, it is helpful to guide them too.

Five Step Processes for Improving Career Decision Making

Finding out how to make use of the right judgment takes knowledge of what kind of decision maker you are, as well as information about yourself , and being familiar with the vast majority of your options. Making choices affects the quality of our lives and impacts our long-term results.

It is usually best to employ a well-organized approach when making major choices. Despite the fact that it's essential to realize that there is no one model that should be used regardless of the way you view it. Choosing the right framework that will allow you to collect facts, consider thoroughly and implement a successful strategy can increase your confidence in making "right" choices.

Certain people settle with decisions based on a compassionate approach such as using the qualities, emotions and considering the impact their decisions will affect other people. Different people use the more authentic or diagnostic approach using, for instance, information, and discerning the benefits as well as the negatives, and then evaluating their circumstances more objectively. Make sure that whichever method you choose to use for settling on decisions , choose which is best for you. Then, consider how you can use it to determine the best decisions.

Correspondence

According to according to the CIP models (Reardon, Lenz, Sampson and Peterson 2005) and using the CASVE approach, the first step in making your vocation is to understand the gap. Being aware of where you are and where you're supposed to go is vital and helps explain the gap. If your anxiety becomes higher than the fear of moving forward than you think, you must make an option. It is vital to acknowledge the need to make a decision and think about the external and internal bits of information. You could identify your problem by describing your situation "I must choose whether to accept this new position or stay at my current place of work for a week." Your inner hints could be enthusiastic, "I am terrified about making the wrong choice." The most important thing is that you are able to see these pieces of information and are familiar with the process of making decisions.

Examining

Examining yourself and your options will allow you to understand what you're looking for. Examining your interests, qualities and abilities will provide some clarity in your own self-analysis. Reviewing your experience through structured activities, evaluation tools as well as other professional resources for direction could be helpful in describing your strengths and passions.

Making improvements to your language-related learning can help you evaluate your options in your research. For instance, obtaining details on different professions or tasks of focus by attending informative meetings, with shadows and organizing understanding, and academic courses will help you learn more about the world of work.

Rememberthat your thoughts affect your mood and behavior and your self-talk may be a positive or negative influence on your decision-making process. the process. Keep your yourself in a positive frame of mind and keep asking an interesting question throughout your journey, like, "What data do I have to contemplate about myself and my circumstances to ensure to prepare myself to come to a conclusion?"

Blend

Being able to distinguish the most extensive number of possible choices in your decision-making process allows you to broaden the scope of this process. Keep in mind that an overly large amount of choices could end dominating your decision making if you do not take a decision by any method. It is important to limit your possible jobs, careers or tasks of focus to a limited number of possibilities to you make your choices. Be aware and consider the ways your preferences align with your assessment of your talents, interests and capabilities.

Esteeming

Analyzing the costs and benefits of each option will aid in reducing the gap you identified in the first stage of this decision-making. For instance, think about yourself family members or other notable people and social gatherings as well as your way of decision-making (legitimate emotional, compassionate, and intuitive) and your assets, such as budgetary commitments (for informative purposes or for preparing alternative options).

To organize your choices It is possible to decide on the most important and optional choices. You can, for instance, make your top choice proviso when it is not feasible due to lack of funds, difficulty in completing an appropriate training or preparation program, or because to changes to your skills or interests (additional period). Be sure to make other options as well.

Execution

Create and implement an agreement to make your first decision. Regardless of whether your agreement includes formal instruction/preparing knowledge, reality-testing (full-time, low maintenance, and humanitarian effort experience) or getting or changing a line of work, it is imperative to build up an arrangement illustrating explicit quantifiable strides with reasonable periods. Be sure to look at the individual and conditions that could influence your approach such as time-related demands as well as family commitments, a sense of anxiety, financial and HR, as well as the way you make decisions.

Making good choices to enhance your vocation or teaching method requires energy, time and ability to execute. Knowing the process of vocation selection and determining a method that you can trust is vital. Making improvements in your abilities through various actions and more knowledgeable about your choices will make a lasting impact on your career taking decisions.

Logic Analyzer - Nothing else works as It

As computers and everything electronic is powered by electricity and electricity, it is important to be aware that every activity depends on the signal: on or off (which is either one or zero for the electrical circuits) for all capabilities. If you need to test a rationale circuit in any of the electronics gadgets it is necessary to have a piece of precision test equipment which is referred to as an analyzer for rationale.

This device tests the logic circuits that are on board of all kinds and will tell you if the circuit is running, with there are no blemishes in the clothing or wiring in the part of the board being tested to test, or that each of the circuits are completed. The analyzer tests are arranged on the rationale path which is being used to refer to. The tests are designed to be non-interfering with the signal - but rather to observe, perhaps, as a man would watching from the sidelines, searching for the correct actions towards the sign being presented; there is no collaboration but rather observing and recording the information. It can be thought of as an uninvolved domain that can only call the play that happens at his feet (yes or not, no or off).

After installing this analyzer's rationale, the system will be tightly for a certain trigger or movement to occur (if it occurs at the moment). ...). If the perfect signal is detected and the data is retrieved and converted into an appropriate arrangement. The company can be found from creating code for get-togethers (recollect the very first computers programming languages?) to the design of graphs that show timing. The data may be captured and transferred through a variety of methods.

If the expert is trained, the specialist who is in question could take this information and work on the framework, or make different actions that result in spot-making using the captured data. (Sounds like something James Bondish, doesn't it?) The specialist will likely identify and pinpoint an area of the identified inconvenience area. After that, you can retest to determine if all of the troublesome areas has been identified and repaired. In a way it can be transformed into an actual game within the game itself or even generation.

Rationale investigation equipment is absolute requirement for any company that provides electrical equipment, to ensure good entertainment or work that relies on perfect rationale circuits for their final product. There are a variety of testing areas in which rationale examination is required to ensure the safety of a product. Find your child's with a hand-held device and uncover the reality of the circuit.

What is an logic Analyzer and why is it necessary for the Digital and Networking Industries?

A rationale analyzer is a type of test equipment that can be used to ensure that an the circuit is functioning in the way it was designed. The rationale analyzer displays the levels of rationale (the parallel numbers 0 and 1) of the circuit, which can be analyzed by a different type of hardware. An oscilloscope isn't able to detect the massive amount of warnings an advanced framework can provide. A rationale analyzer is collecting data that isn't detected by other method.

A rationale examination device is part of the modern framework that includes a series of tests. In the past, when they first came out to be used, they were attached to a large number of clasps, however in the course of a few years the introduction of rationale tests was made into use across the board. They guarantee a safe relationship, which is both precisely and electrically. They're specifically designed to be as easy as possible to keep the electrical sign unchanged. After setting the rationale analyzer then the trigger condition is established. A trigger condition could be anything that is triggered, from activating an exact HTTP parcel to activating on the edge of an indication. When the data is gathered by the analyzer's program, it can transform it into various arrangements. These companies can range beyond the low-level computing constructs and timing graphs. An expert trained in the field can access this data converted and utilize it to study computers and their framework.

Rationale investigation equipment is employed extensively in the computers that make chips and in the systems management projects. Rationale analyzers are an all out requirement for any business that is dependent on an exact chip configuration according to plan or a system that is running efficiently.

Problem of Problem Solving Problem of Problem Solving

The majority of people who are not experts on the phrase Logic Analyser might struggle to understand what the device is, or what the benefits to the user of using one.

To make it easier to comprehend For ease of understanding, an Analyser is a simple device to comprehend. Analyser is an element of electronic equipment that can display signals within the most sophisticated circuit. It measures the voltage of a "rationale" electronic signal that might in some way or other be too rapid to even take into consideration the measurement.

Although Logic analyzers appear similar to oscilloscopes numerous differences that make each one of them suitable for a range of jobs and for estimating requirements.

Once the data is gathered by the analyzer, it can be changed over it into a range of companies for convenience, exploration, and more research. The information can also be transferred to various fragile and sensitive PCs.

The Varieties

Due to the huge number of jobs and requirements for an analyzer of rationale There are three main versions available on the market.

They are classified in unmistakable categories.

Centralized server Analysers think of an entity that can include the display, the controls, PC as well as space to install the equipment required. The showcase can be customized by the user according to their specific requirements and needs.

Independent units are those that are made ready for use with various projects installed during the assembly stage.

The other option is PC-based analyzers, which include equipment that is connected to the PC by an YSB or Ethernet connection. The PC then receives the information and saves it for analysis and estimation.

The fourth (half or half) option are analyzers that are referred to by the name blended signal oscilloscopes. They combine the components of the two pieces of machine to make it easier for users of the user.

The Logic Analyser you choose to be used for a particular purpose

One of the limitations of normal oscillators and rationale analyzers is the lack of memory and screen space which could assist clients with studying and exam.

The vast majority of these devices are used by experts who would like to capture and save their data, as well as analyze it in the near future for purposes of inconvenience shooting as well as for inquiries into logical reasoning It is no wonder that a few handheld devices have been found to be insufficient to be used for this purpose.

In any event the use of an analyzer that required the programming or equipment of the standard "screen as well as tower" PC would have suggested that their usage was to being unintelligible in the field of work, especially when it involved harsh terrain or the transfer of space from space.

The advancements in workstation and hand-held processing has led to advancements in the technology utilized to produce and manufacture rationale analyzers that can be modified to fit the latest and modern PCs, offering the best of both universes in an efficient and flexible packaging, yet allowing all the benefits of the device to degrade, shoot and then settle on a few options out in the field.

What does problem-solving mean:

Problem-solving is primarily an intellectual process of thinking by individuals. The behavior of problem-solving can be observed generally under extreme conditions. Any activity, an person has a goal to complete at any cost. With the help of deterrents to achieve the goal, a problem occurs. The reason for the obstacle may be attitudinal or physical or social, or financial based. Whatever the case it's an enthusiastic and active specialist who is working to hinder the progress of the person. In these situations the solution is not possible using conventional methods and strategies. The person has the option to try a different approach to address the issue. But, a wealth of information on the human condition could help to make a quick arrangement. In this particular issue this issue, the topic is important in the related areas.

Problem situations of all kinds:

Specific and general

Straightforward, but confused

From the inside and outside

There is there is no arrangement

Self-solving, assisted by others and supported by others

Whatever it is issues should be solved at any cost with just a little effort and clear confidence. If not, the person must endure a loss of serenity. In some instances, it could be difficult to come up with an answer. However there is no way recommended to resign from the work of implementing the solution. In that case the method of solving problems should be considered.

Logical strides to solve problems:

The process of solving problems shouldn't be random and unplanned. It needs estimates of the ventures to be carried out using the same methodological approach. There are seven phases that could be made up of:

The conscious awareness of the issue is the primary way to perceive the issue. It occurs every occasionally that a problem doesn't get noticed when it first begins. In the course of time one becomes conscious of the issue, seeking a solution. The person is simply observing and logical the proximity of a issue. There is no way of identifying and understanding the issue.

Determining the issue At this point the problem can be analyzed to allow for an appreciation. When identifying and categorizing the issue, a clear understanding is created and data is accumulated that provides an ideal understanding of the issue. This is the very first step in which the person concerned is looking into the issue.

Collecting relevant data information Data that is relevant is collected from any reliable source that is relevant to the issue. In all the time, reliable tools like magazines and books have been cited.

Specification of speculation: This is the process of creating the game strategy. After analyzing the issue and gathering information, a variety of possible projects are planned. The person is allowed to advise others if they in addition to having experiences, knowledge or other capabilities when it comes to establishing the fundamental plans to solve the issue efficiently.

Evaluation of the theory The sample plans are taken to be evaluated by using them in training to solve the issue. Each conditional arrangement is thoroughly examined and an appraisal is made. The most appropriate and final decision is based on the correctness of the outcome or results.

Checking the arrangement of decision: The validity of the arrangement chosen for the activity is checked using the similar arrangement in finding solutions to the problem in the next as well as other comparable questions. If they're found to be reasonable in addressing every question, then it is recognized as the correct arrangement to solve the issue at hand.

Making a new arrangement if it is not successful If the plan chosen for the task is insufficient for all purposes and purposes to solve the problem of the current issue The opportunity exists to make a choice from the list of options the moment.

The challenge of problem-solving

As we've seen the ability to solve problems isn't as effective as a firework of correct arrangement. Be cautious at every step of the process, from defining, to analysis as well as verification before making the final decision. Other than that, repeated regrets, will solution to the current problem , while reverting to a different option will be unwise.

In this way, solving problems is without doubt thought of as a challenge. In such a situation only experience and relationships techniques can be very helpful.

Chapter 4: Mental Models As Well As Self-Discipline

Everyone is disgusted by the term "discipline." The mere mention or the mere thought by itself can trigger tears and shrugs. As we imagine discipline, it is easy to often think of taking joy away from ourselves. If we imagine discipline, we envision self-deprivation to do tasks we don't really like to do. But what if we did not think of discipline as a form of punishment? What if we saw it as a method to reach our goals, making more simple to reach to where we want to go, and help make our day more enjoyable?

In reality, setting up self-disciplined habits can reduce stress, help you achieve your desires and goals Make time for the things you love, enhance relations, and ultimately make you an overall more successful and happier person. We believe that self-discipline does not have any relevance to our everyday lives after we've reached adulthood However, some of the habits of successful people actually depend heavily on self-discipline.

Things like waking up at the right time, exercising and practicing good dental hygiene as well as maintaining your relationships (both at workplace and in your private lives) all require a bit of self-control. The discipline of self-control can improve every aspect of your life, such as friendships, health, relationships with your partner, mental illness such as depression and anxiety, at school and work and much other things.

It might be surprising however, often our greatest struggles are directly linked to our inability to manage ourselves. If you're sleeping all night the night before a big presentation, and resenting your self for not being prepared in the weeks prior to it, you're not good at the ability to manage your time. It's obviously an ability that requires self-control to develop. If you're in a rocky financial situation and you're unable to get out of the cycle of living paycheck-to-paycheck , and have an unimaginably inadequate savings accounts (or no savings at all) it could be because you're not self-control. A life that isn't self-disciplined (or even with a lack of self-control) is really living on the high-road.

A life of self-discipline that has strong behaviors can be an extremely successful one. Self-discipline is being able to arrange your schedule in a way that are a source of nourishment for every aspect of your wellbeing including time for work, time with your family and friends, as well as time for you. Self-discipline is living with less stress because you believe that you've completed everything that needs to be accomplished instead of giving it up for your future self tidy up the mess. How can you start to establish self-discipline in your daily life? Through mental models, naturally.

The Eisenhower Matrix

It's been said before that time management is crucial. What is the reason? having habits that aid in managing your time effectively can lead to a higher self-esteem and more satisfaction at school and work as well as higher respectability and better relationships, among others. The ability to eliminate your list of tasks consistently results in feelings of achievement and confidence.

You'll enjoy reaching the end of your day, and will be more motivated to start your day in the morning day when you hear your self-talk sound similar to, "I can do this! I was a success yesterday!". Professionally, you'll be more successful by having time management skills, regardless of what it looks as for your. Being able to prioritize your projects in order to meet deadlines and also be able to devote time to the projects is vital to the success of your workplace.

People will notice when you improve your performance as well, and you'll be admired and appreciated as a friend. Management of time also results in happier partners and family members. If you are able to balance your work, goals and various other tasks You'll focus more on the beloved ones and allowing them to enjoy the time they deserve while you're in their company.

Despite all the benefits of time management yet, many individuals struggle to establish the habits that are required to keep it. It's too difficult to handle or they are too busy to take time to organize and prioritize. People who do not take the an effort to organize their day but suffer more than those who do. The lack of time management skills are typically linked to higher rates of anxiety, stress and depression.

People who don't organize their schedules accordingly, don't sleep as much, or sleep as long, and experience an endless whirlwind of work in their minds when they finally close. They struggle to balance their home and work lives which affects their relationship as a result of it.

Time management is a disciplined process and it doesn't happen in a flash. It is, however, achievable for anyone willing to do the effort to master this ability, practice these practices, and live a living a more fulfilling, happier life. It begins with learning to prioritize.

There are few greater examples of life that are productive than the presidency of Dwight D. Eisenhower. In his two terms in the presidency of 34th President the president Eisenhower initiated programs to establish an infrastructure of highways within the United States, launch the internet, and also explore the outer space through NASA.

But it's not the only thing. Before Eisenhower was president of the United States, he was also a Commanding General for the Allied Forces during World War II and General with five stars in the Army as well as being the very first Chief of Staff for NATO at the time of 1951. He was also the President of Columbia University. It's also been said that he had time to relax by playing golf or oil painting. It's safe for us to say that President Eisenhower had plenty to do (and was able to manage it).

The most potent (and most user-friendly) instruments for managing time is called the Eisenhower Matrix, also known as the Eisenhower Box. The mental model is set to blow your task list over the top. Applying this concept to your self-discipline tools will force you to reconsider how you organize your time.

Urgent Not Urgent

Important Do

Take action now. Make a decision now.

Set it up for the future.

Not important Delegate

Do you think someone else could help me? Do you want to delete it?

Eliminate it.

As you can observe it, as you will see, the Eisenhower Matrix breaks tasks down into four distinct categories or boxes. These categories are classified by urgency to not-so-urgent, and from important to not so crucial. The first category that is located within the box's upper left hand corner, is"Do First "Do First" category.

They are among some of the urgent, crucial tasks on your to-do list, and they should to be completed as quickly as is possible. The tasks of this kind include things like having an appointment filled with prescriptions or finishing your work on a project due in the near future. Anything that must not be delayed for too long should be put in this category. President Eisenhower states that setting a deadline and performing these tasks as quickly as possible is the most effective way to go about it.

The second category, the one located in the upper right-hand corner is where you'll find crucial, but less urgent, tasks such as The

"Decide" category. These are items on the to-do list which are essential to get done , but will have to be left until longer to be completed. These tasks could be things like having your oil changed or folding your laundry that's still at the foot of the bed.

Things that need to be done quickly but don't have an end date (or have deadlines that are coming but isn't imminent) are best placed into this box. The items included in"Decide" box are tasks that need to be completed quickly. Items in "Decide" category are items that must be scheduled to complete at a particular date in the near future. Be sure to put the date aside and add it to your planner or calendar to make sure this task doesn't get delayed any longer than is necessary.

The third box in the lower left-hand edge is"Delegate "Delegate" Box. This is a category of tasks which require time however they are not as critical and may be handed on to another person for completion.

The goal of these categories is to identify that projects do not necessarily require your attention, but they do require your attention. For instance, if you are involved in a particular one or two category task and your husband contacts you to ask if you'd like to take pet food for him on your return journey, you could provide him with the required details (the type of dog food you would like) to finish the task by himself, or delegate an assignment in the category of three to another person. One thing you should remember in this particular category is that you must be aware of who you delegated the task to in order to follow up with the person you delegated it to when you need to.

The third category is reserved for tasks that aren't urgent nor important The tasks that fall into this category belong to the "Eliminate" box. Items that fall into"Eliminate "Eliminate" category will get impeding your productivity and hinder the ability of you to finish tasks from those in the second, first and third categories. They could be harmful behaviors, such as scrolling through social media or tasks that consume the time of others and do not need to be done currently, such as buying new shoes for your work to go to the store.

This is a category that may require the greatest amount of discipline because it requires you to tell yourself "no" for yourself whenever you're looking to engage in activities that don't contribute to your productivity. However, this doesn't mean that the things you enjoy to do in your spare time, that aren't geared towards work like watching TV or reading can't be put in this category.

The purpose of managing time is to manage your time between your work and personal life to make space to complete the tasks you'd like to accomplish. This is a category for the things on your list agenda that just take up space, and aren't really time-sensitive or crucial currently. Keep in mind that your primary resource is time.

Strategies for using The Eisenhower Box:

Limit the number of tasks you assign to each quadrant. If you have five tasks in each quadrant, you must complete the most crucial or time-sensitive task within the "Do" category. Don't try to accumulate tasks. You're looking to finish them.

Use only one list for all aspects within your daily life (business homework, personal and family, etc.) So you don't have to fret about not completing one list and another.

Don't let anyone determine what your priorities ought to be. It is your checklist to control your time and you must write it out with your eyes on the ball.

BJ Fogg's Small Habits Mental Model

Have you considered making a major change or committing to a huge target, but then given up because you thought that you wouldn't be able to achieve it? If you had an audience this moment and someone was asking this question, every single person's hand would be up in the air. It happens to everyone.

It's easy to become disillusioned when something you'd like to achieve appears to be an unattainable enormous, incredibly huge deal. It's even more difficult to take a massive ambition like that, and break it into smaller pieces so that you can figure out what to do next. Perhaps you've been trying to shed the last 30 pounds for a while but you've decided to give up. You might really want to return to school but you're overwhelmed by the process of making it happen. Maybe you're exhausted of feeling unworthy and want to take a leap of self-love but don't know where to start or how to be able to access the resources this. Every person at one point or one time or another is in that position. It's all too overwhelming.

BJ Fogg, director of the Lab for Behavior located at Stanford University, was right exactly where you are. Fogg studied behavioral science for over two decades but one day, he discovered he was at a dead end during his quest to shed weight. He started to play around, using the knowledge he had gained about the behavior of people, to help jolt himself from this rut and to get back on track with losing the weight he'd hoped to lose at the start of his journey. He purchased an electronic scale in the hope that stepping onto it daily and seeing the numbers would inspire him to keep going. But it did not. He began logging his weight and daily calories on Twitter each morning to determine if this could help. It did not.

He realized that just three things can change your the way you behave being able to recognize an epiphany altering your surroundings or taking a single step. Based on these two concepts, Fogg developed his Tiny Habits Method, an easily accessible mental model to help you develop self-control.

Fogg's Tiny Habits Method is centered on making a tiny step towards a massive target each day at one day at. This may sound like a lot of work, but it's not. It's true. But it's effective. When it is followed this mental model, it can produce lasting, long-lasting results by altering behavior in tiny increments according to the name.

The first step is a similar to that of the First Principles mental model we were introduced to via Elon Musk. We'll begin by thinking about the desired outcome we'd like to achieve (for Fogg, it was losing weight). We'll then go backwards to think about the habits which lead to the desired result, and then reduce them gradually until we come to a easy to modify to help achieve the desired outcomes. To reduce weight it could be increasing the amount of water consumed or reducing stress levels exercising or any other variety of habits. You can then pick one small habit to develop into a routine. For Fogg this was push-ups.

In the next step, Fogg asserts, you must realize that your behavior succeed it must be accompanied by the desire to perform it as well as the capability to carry out it, and lastly, an event (or an invitation to action) to carry out the action. The last one is vital and the call to action is most effective when it's something you do on a regular basis regardless. You don't need to work extra hard or make a special effort to accomplish. Following these guidelines Fogg decided to get his desired result of losing weight Fogg would perform two push-ups each when he used the bathroom.

That's right. Each time he flushed after going to the bathroom throughout his daytime hours, he fell to the ground and did two push-ups. It's crazy, doesn't it? As if it could never be effective? Doing push-ups every when he went to the bathroom on a daily basis, Fogg lost five pounds in the first week, then ten and then twenty pounds over the course of a couple of months. It's a real success.

What does this mean to you? What can you do to make these mental models and testing it out aid you in achieving greater self-control? First, if you establish an unintentional habit and stay in it for a few months or even weeks and you'll see the fruits of the goals you've set. You'll lose weight or write a book, or get rid of the habit of drinking coffee.

What else can you do? Beginning a small habit and sticking to it can also help you gain the opportunity to develop and stay in new routines that's healthy for you. The first step to self-discipline is identifying practices that are beneficial to you in the long run , and following through with determination to keep working on these behaviors. As time passes you'll gain confidence in yourself and motivation to be successful. It will be clear how your achievement (or even your failure) is yours to determine. It's your decision whether you achieve your goals or not. It's not fate or luck that is responsible for your accomplishment. It's your dedication to work and perseverance that will carry you to the end of the road.

Tips for using The Tiny Habits Method:

Watch BJ Fogg's presentation at TedxFremont on YouTube.

Pick a goal that you're enthusiastic about and determined to get there. It's important to be committed to it!

Choose a behavior you're able to do.

Select the trigger (or call-to-action for the behavior you perform all the time making it simpler for you to perform the action.

Pick a behavior that is small enough to be acceptable.

Invite a person to share your experience or create their own little habit with you

Celebrate! You're on the way!

Re-visit the goals you set when you started studying this text. Do any linked to self-discipline issues? What could you do using your Eisenhower Matrix or the Tiny Habits Method to correct the problem? Keep these both mental models within your your mind during your week can help you build discipline that makes you a happier and prosperous person. But, they are just two of the many mental models available which help build self-discipline practices. Conduct some research on your own to discover new mental models that can aid you in this process also.

Keep in mind that self-discipline is a virtue that manifests its presence in every aspect of life. If you get yourself up from your bed each morning instead of to snooze again on your alarm and again, you're practicing self-discipline. When you gather with a friend for an honest discussion about an argument that you have had earlier in the week instead of trying to avoid the conflict you're practicing self-control. Recognize the little victories and give yourself a pat on the back when you realize that you've adhered to a practice that leads to improved self-control. It's possible!

Chapter 5: Mental Modeling Things You Should Know About Chain Thought

Meditation is the act of recognizing the mind with the aim of following your own thought Chains to develop a practical Mental Model.

Our minds are always changing. While we interact with our surroundings our minds are developing mental chains of thought. The result is a constant roar of noise. It's like the radio station that is set to the same channel that plays in your head for forever. If you don't have the benefit of the control of volume or an off switch, you're lost. Yoga and meditation give you the control of volume as well as an on-off switch to use when you need to.

A majority of our ideas and activities result out of the thought chain. We are the things we think. Therefore, it follows that we must consider understanding how our mind works by observing how our minds function, as something important that deserves our close attention to.

Repetition is necessary which is what Meditation does. It is a procedure that is based on a functioning model of the way our minds function. Meditation is a method that allows us to become our minds to work. Through Meditation you can:

Check out your own ideas,

Take a look at your ideas from an perspective of the observer and the person you have watched

* Find ways to alter your thinking and become more successful,

You must realize that your way of thinking and interact with others, determines the kind of person you are. Lastly,

Recognize the many physical and mental benefits yoga and Meditation provides.

Mental movements trigger thoughts that are linked with different opinions.

Thus, the fundamental collaboration with the environment is what triggers an process. This is typically the case. The first thing you do is react to someone who is reminiscent of Bob. You respond to the external environmental change. The observer, you then proceed to observe the increase and then react. This triggers another idea, perception, and response as well as another again.

You can even construct thought chains that could ultimately result in a completely unexpected idea or topic. For example:

* You begin to notice the person who is reminiscent of Bob,

You are aware how much you "like" Bob,

* Bob makes you feel good,

You might consider, "Bob was always fit as fiddle, he played a lot,"

* You consider you claim physical molding,

You can see that you're not thrilled about the body you're in.

* This can make you feel uneasy,

You're thinking, "I need to get to the fitness center and exercise more."

* You look at the screen, and you feel great, but you don't have the energy to make it to the recreation center today, because you have to be at work later,

* At this point, you notice that you don't feel enough and you're not likely to workout today, during the evening hours.

In the above thought-chain you left the main idea, and you may have observed that you felt good, then feeling terrible, to feeling great, and then being miserable again in a matter of minutes. Wow! Insane right.

But, it is the thing we do regularly. We are constantly exposed to this unproductive mental trance. Beginning with one thought chain and then the next frequently , without paying attention to what's happening around our minds.

There is no way you can stop the problem, modify it, or else, not let the negative impact on your life. Sometimes, you'll go on , without even acknowledging what you do.

With Yoga and Meditation Through Yoga and Meditation, you'll discover ways to filter your thought patterns and identify irrelevant mechanical evidence in your reasoning. You will construct a realistic model of your mind's capabilities work, with the aim that you will be able to detect negative thought chains and begin to develop new positive thoughts to replace them. You will continue to push forward in your daily life and make your ideal life that is vibrant and fulfilling.

Mental Models The Box Everyone is Thinking Outside of

How often is a person in business hearing, "It's a great opportunity to think outside the thinking?"" The mental models represent the trap that everyone is trying to get out of. Mental models block thinking forward situations. Personal perspectives are developed through discernment, creativity mind and appreciation of the world around us. A person sees the candy bar and is sure that it's a candy, or is it actually a mobile phone sporting candy bar cases? The unique phone case was an ideal moment to think ahead because it was able to deconstruct an imaginary model. The most prominent use for mental model is help shape an individual's view of his self in relation to the surroundings. Self-images are constructed by apparent capabilities, social activities and training. A lot of this self-image triggers subconscious beliefs.

Human beliefs are a part of the business. The majority of businesses thrive by staying ahead of their competition and understand that if negligence takes over the competitive edge can be lost. The assumptions of business leaders result in ease, which makes it easier to navigate the reality. In many cases, these assumptions leave organizations stuck in the same spot when development is cruising through. This phenomenon is most prevalent in big multi-channel businesses as employees are immersed in the corporate mission that is more prominent. International organizations with cross-lattice, particularly have earned a reputation for having been able to come to an agreement. "This is the way it's always been done" is repeated time and repeatedly as companies are unable to take a slice of the pie due to hidden competition and the advancement.

The tale of the huge business that fails to notice groundbreaking moments and is debunked by the small but deft contestant is presented repeatedly and over again in business colleges. The solution to the problem of childish beliefs is a part of outside-of-the-box thinking. Outside of the box thinking is able to help the most reputable organizations become more agile in their leadership. Human beings are inherently flawed and need help in predicting future business slants due to preconceived mental models. The image of

67

competition surrounding the company, which employees build, is just an example. The most obvious choice for every company is to choose out of the box to provide protection against negligence and brand value mishaps and wear and tear on clients.

Don't wait until you require the Corporate Emergency Response.

Sometimes the most unusual way a business could do is seek outside help in the development of a better type of alternative. Outside of the business, but the marketplace. While your business or company requires an expert in development You also need one who understands the importance of the foundation and as a venture stone and not a rethink.

Each business and industry has their own distinct culture and this culture is often the cause of an underlying "customary subjective visual impairment." Similar ideas keep popping out because the same people are charged with finding new solutions to the same old problems. In all likelihood over the long term the company either grows its operations to the highest position in the market or it is unable to make and eventually goes into the process of liquidation.

Understanding Choices and Decision Making

The term "Decision" also known as "Decision-making" is perhaps one of the oldest well-known terms in the field of human development. The concept of decision-making has been around from the beginning of time, despite the fact that people were not aware about the conscious act that included a myriad of ideas and assessments. In fact, even the stone man was making decisions when he decided to create a few tools for the next dinner he would serve. In the course of a long period, the thinking mind of humans became more organized, and people began seeking proofs before coming to resolutions. The perspective was progressively rational, more based on examination and a search action that was pushed out beyond the boundaries of exploratory research.

In the present, as the world sits in the midst of many political and financial changes, we're talking about decisions unlike ever before. In any case it is a chance or plan to move forward into the next stage of decision-making should not come in the broad sphere of the audience or come with a handful of financial or money-related political implications. It is usually something that is extremely personal, such as selecting an exclusive brand or undertaking a specific work. Even as board Gurus discuss "successful decision-making" and enhancing the "Decision-making capabilities" of their employees The human element of every process must be considered.

Making Decisions: The science of making a decision isn't grasped until we know what exactly is an actual decision, what is an decision " an achievable one" as well as the consequences that come with making a "terrible option."

It is your decision to make at the time you make a decision. Additionally, you make a decision after you reach an agreement. But, making a decision isn't as simple. It is an intricate three-dimensional process. Three dimensions make the process of making decisions extremely fascinating and captivating.

* The psychological aspect The psychological dimension of decisions cannot be understood without a connection. They should be

evaluated according to the human need and values, as well as business demands, and their conditions.

* Cognitive dimension: No decision is conclusive. The constantly changing requirements of a company following certain time frames can challenge the credibility of certain decisions. As requirements change the process of making decisions is viewed as a process that is never-ending, inexplicably ever-changing, and constantly evolving.

* Logical Dimension A decision can be rational and reasonable, or absurd and untrue. However, a rational method of making informed decisions is based on a rational and solid methodology, not an overly enthusiastic and silly approach.

While the decision-making process is scientifically based, the importance of the human instinct in decision-making shouldn't be denied.

When we discuss the process of making decisions we are talking about the framework that is logically tied. In the future, we will talk about the smallest possible set of outcomes that are quantifyable.

In the end, all decisions should not be based on science that is:

The decision-making process is based on the political or bureaucratic expert.

The decision-making process is based on flipping the coin, tarot cards or Supplication gatherings

This includes simply following instructions

The decisions are made without much thought

In our modern world the ability to make decisions is a highly praised skill. Many businesses pay a particular attention to this when it comes to the ability to pursue or enroll.

Instead of logical and well-informed decision-making, the choices that each and every one of us takes in each moment of our lives are often uninformed and "on off the cuff" choices.

There are people in our society who make important decisions.

* Someone with an open and tolerant mind. Someone with a closed mind will not come up with amazing choices. In the mind of the

person it is as if they've just sketched an exact strategy. For these people who are not formal decision makers, is not even a reality. it's only an effect. For those who are not legally able to, the scientific process of decision-making is working in vain. It is not lucrative assets.

* The ability to share data: Anyone who is open to look into. However you should be willing to put effort into data. An informed decision that is not backed by solid information is a misrepresentation.

* Imagined mind: Someone with an open mind who is keen to invest resources into top quality information must be able to anticipate the outcomes of his or her decisions.

Are you looking to step out in a different direction Someone who is afraid of the consequences of bad choices may not be able to make the right choices.

Determination Making: The Bridge Between Failure & Success

Decision making is the foundation of any business or administration move. A better management decision-making process and problem-solving could dramatically enhance the organization's outcomes and benefits.

However studies show that Managers and Entrepreneurs do not attain more than half of the correct outcomes when it comes to decision making and solving problems.

In the present tense business climate the ability to make decisions is one of the most significant tests administered by authority. The ability to make decisions differentiates between a weak and good pioneer. Many bad choices are made because pioneers move through the decision-making process too fast and are unable to put together the ends of emotions, bad data, or even the driving factors.

Before we begin to talk more about it, I'd like to present to you an amazing tale about decision-making, that shows us how skilled our managers are when it comes to decision making!

Let's Touch is about a leader of a large company who was struck by a heart attack and a specialist suggested he travel for a few weeks to a farm to ease the tension. The man visited a ranch and after a couple of days, he felt exhausted. He requested the farmer to assign him a task to complete.

The farmer was able to guide him through the process of cleaning the shit that the animals had. He believed those who are from cities living a full time in an office that it would take for seven days in order to finish the task, but to his surprise management, the boss completed the job in just one day.

The next day, the farmer gave the manager a more difficult task: cutting head of 500 chickens. The farmer knew that the manager would not complete the task but by the time the day came to an conclusion, the task was completed.

The next morning, after the majority of jobs at the homestead were completed, the farm owner demanded the manager to put the potatoes into two containers: one with small potatoes, and the other that contained large potatoes.

The day was over the farmer noticed that the manager was seated in front of the potato sack. But the two boxes were empty. The manager was questioned by a the farmer "How did you get to the point where you had such a difficult job during the first days of your career, and you're unable to do this simple job?"

The manager said: "Tune in, for my entire life , I've been making heads, and I'm managing crap and yet you're now asking me to make decisions!! "

Jokes apart, this might be the case for a significant majority of our entrepreneurs and Managers. When the decision-making process is a bit overwhelming or the stakes that are at stake are too significant, we often do not have the slightest clue or don't know which option to pick. If you're a manager or Entrepreneur, there are times when we have all the information we know. There are times when we can be certain of something however, not everything is important. In addition, we may do not know anything at all - even so, we must pick!

Good decision-making is a necessary the process of thinking. And thinking is a key human trait. The primary challenge of thinking is confusion. We try to do many things with the help of two. The emotions, the information and rationality, expectations, and creativity all pile up on us. It's like playing with numerous balls.

There may be some extraordinary plans that have been thought about and formulated in amazing detail, but in the event that we do not pursue it, they could prove useless for us, but instead sad reminders of sitting in a trance, wasting opportunities and unrealized goals.

Therefore, a good decision isn't an accident It is always the result of high ambition determination, proper effort, sharp handling, and a skillful execution. It is a sign of the smart choice of many possibilities. The most significant aspect of decision-making abilities is practicing and understanding high-decision-making systems. Let me give you a few simple steps to make a decision:

1.) Define requirements: All the items that need to be resolved don't seem to be insignificant. In the same way, as we organize the time executives spend when they are seated, we rank how important the choices that we must make. By establishing requirements, we'll be heading towards a direction. If it turns out to be an unintentional route, we're able to adjust the course.

2.) Make a time-line The decision-making process is akin to gut instinct. Also, faster is better. Be 80 percent accurate first and the first instead of 100 percent correct and last.

By setting a deadline that we think about the due date and decide.

3.) Collect and examine state-of-the-art and cold, concrete facts However, you must collect numerous facts that could be expected in the current circumstances but not many. Create these. Based on the requirement to wait until the situation is perfect as we've got all data possible, or we have to make a decision based on our experience.

4.) Draw a picture of the desired outcome What do we in the ideal world require? If we've not looked at it, by how can we tell what we'll get?

5.) Compare the advantages against the disadvantages of getting to the place we want to be there are exchanges, and settlements. Consider the costs and impact.

6.) Consider the implications for everyone involved Who is affected? Learn the effects of the choices we make on the individuals affected.

7.) Be sure to keep emotions out of it: Do not allow our emotions influence our decisions, no matter how much is reasonable.

8.) Utilize our shrewdness, be fearless, follow our gut feeling and make the choice procrastination in the name of reducing risk creates risk. If the method of expository is different from our capabilities, we must put aside the task of making sense of the reason why the distinction is there. It's likely to be a case of going by instinct, but regardless we considered the diagnostic method.

9) Make the decision without doubt: Transform the decision into specific strategies. Follow our agreement.

10.) Review the results of our decision as well as the actions to take What kind of exercises could be completed? This is a crucial move to further develop our ability to make decisions and our judgment.

Many times, making decisions might not be as easy as we imagine and it could be difficult if it involves a number of conflicts or frustration. The challenge is to select one option where the positive result is more likely to be better than the negative. Remaining in a absence from the decisions you make regularly seems to be the most straightforward. However be, remember that making our own decisions and accepting the consequences is the most effective way to be accountable for our lives as well as our business's success.

Chapter 6: Individual And Collective Mental Models Beware, Automatic Routines Are Inflecible!

A mental model is a collection of assumptions, meanings and rules of reasoning inferences, etc. that can lead us to form the right decision about what we should interpret. According to Peter Senge puts it, "they are deeply-rooted in assumptions, generalizations, images of stories, pictures or images that affect our ways of thinking about and acting in our world." They function continuously subconsciously, in our private life as well as in our professional world of our institutions, assisting us in giving an understanding to the world and work efficiently. Mental models are the basis for all of our actions and interpretations. They are the way we think, feel and feel, think and interact.

Mental models that differ from one another can trigger different thoughts, feelings or opinions. They can also influence actions. For instance, for an accountant, a particular outcome of a business is indicating stability and must continue its course. For the vice-president of marketing, this result indicates that the company is not growing and it's time to start with a fresh marketing campaign. If a member of the board this is that "disapproval" of CEO policies. For investors it means that it's time to sell shares. For another, it's the time to invest. The outcome is the same. The world's environment is exactly the same. what is the reason for the different results are the various mental models.

Different perspectives, beliefs and actions aren't an issue in and of themselves. They can become contradictory, in the sense that everyone thinks that their method of looking at the world (according according to the mental models they have) will be the sole way to see them, or at the very least the one that is "reasonable." Naturally, this notion that there is "rationality" can be an opinion that is shaped by the mental model of every person. Everyone believes that their own model is the best one. Instead of using different perspectives to expand their perspective and blend the different perspectives into a common understanding Each of the participants stick to their particular viewpoint. Instead of challenging the logic of the other person to discover his mental model, participants engage in a struggle to determine who is the "right" view of reality.

Mental models also comprise the file that includes routine behavior. As we've seen when beginning a new exercise (such like driving in a vehicle for instance) one must be aware of making random decisions. However, as time goes by as the practice progresses, the brain develops the ability to perform actions automatically, passing those decisions to the subconscious and benefiting from the benefits of what Gregory Bateson calls "the habit economy." This is vital to the human condition because, without it, there would be no way to move at the speed that is required by the circumstances. But it comes with one cost: automated routines are not flexible.

The rigidity of the habit is essential to operate efficiently in stable environments. Much like the autopilot in an aircraft, this habit of a human pilot allows him to focus on other aspects. But using autopilot when during the storm can be risky. The inability to adapt to changing contexts is one of the primary reasons for the extinction of species (such such as the dinosaurs) or agriculture (such such as Roman) and businesses (99 from 100 companies go out of business in the first ten years, while the estimated average life span for Fortune 500 companies is less than 40 years) as well as families (60 percent of marriages across the world end with divorce) and even people (according to the latest data 50 percent of deaths prior to age 40 could be attributable to the behavior of people).

The filters humans organize our lives and interpret our experiences are drawn in four different sources: biology culture, language, and personal history. The four main sources define the "usual" reaction to specific conditions, based on your mental model. In order to shed more illumination about the four sources that we briefly mentioned before I'll attempt to explain these sources in the next paragraphs:

Biology

The primary filter for cognitive models comes from the brain. We are afflicted by physical limitations that hinder us from seeing certain things with our senses. The human ear for instance is between 20 and 20 to 20,000 vibrations per second however dogs detect more subtle shades, and for elephants can hear more serious sounds. Night vision for humans is not as good as that of felines as well as our vision at distance is much less than the vision of a hawk. It is a matter of distance from which humans are capable of seeing directly the frequencies that lie between 680 and 380 millimeters which is a small part of the spectrum of electromagnetic frequencies.

The inability to perceive implies that it is impossible to take action. When a dog responds to an ultrasonic whistling sound however, the human can't even know it is there. When the bat is operating in total darkness, one is lost. This is why we, the human race create instruments like radar and sonar to extend the perception capabilities of our senses, and ultimately, our ability to be able to move.

Our relationship with the world is far more complex than we realize. The theory of perception objective claims that what happens "out there" causes immediate changes and causes changes to the brain "in this moment." The theory is challenged by Humberto Maturana as well as Francisco

Varela argue that the outside world only causes disruptions to the system of nerves. Perceptual perception is influenced more by the structure of their nervous system, rather than due to any external disturbance. The authors of The Tree of Knowledge, Maturana and Varela establish that the brain is an enclosed system. This concept is contrary to the conventional belief that it is defined to be "an instrument that gathers information from the surrounding environment and creates a representation of the world that the body utilizes to determine the best behavior to ensure its existence. According to Maturana and Variela" Insofar as biological and human cognitive systems concern, the complete experience of life is in us, and there is nothing that is outside of our perception.

This theory explains how everyone sees the same picture when they gaze at something, even though no one can see the world around them for themselves. The commonality of our biological structure allows us to function within a shared reality. Maturana and Varela both affirm that what a person experiences can be described as "(reality)" instead of "reality." As written in brackets "(reality)" refers to the experience that is experienced within the field of energy that are external and inaccessible, that we refer to as "reality" in the absence of parentheses. We are in an intersubjective (reality) but it is not due to the fact that what we see as (reality) we experience is the true outside world, however, the external environment triggers similar reactions within our brains and nervous systems.

Language

The second filter in the mental model we have is the language. The language is the medium by which the the human being is organized. Language is the place of meaning, where the reality is described as comprehensible and understandable. With the help of the language we are able to communicate with each other and with others about what is in the world around us and inside us.

The most common perception of the language can be described as "label theorem." Based on this concept, people perceive things around us as they are , and then give them a name, or an identification. This is the main function of language as the descriptive system used for classification and labeling preexisting, and, consequently, independent perceptions. This theory is not complete and only explains only a small part of the function of the language. Researchers studying cognition the brain, consciousness, and cognition have concluded that language classifications are not labels that apply to perceptions that already exist; on contrary, they condition and define perception in the first place by ensuring that the individual doesn't talk about what he perceives and only perceives the things he is able to talk about.

An accountant "watches" on the balance sheet what mechanical engineers do not observe. However, the engineer may not see the exact numbers; however, He does lack the distinctions accounting (the language) must interpret these numbers. The mechanical engineer is able to "read" the system of differential equations that are completely unintelligible to the meters. The accountant may not see the same signals but he doesn't have the distinctions that an engineer (the language) is required to understand those signals. The ability to distinguish and to organize the world into functional categories is what's known as "intelligence."

Culture

The third major source of mental models is the culture. Culture can be thought of as a mental model that is collective. According to Edgard Schein states, "culture is a pattern of common assumptions that are learned by a group in the process of overcoming their issues of external adaptation and integration within the group. The proof of this particular pattern of assumptions is successful can be seen in the fact that this pattern has performed well enough to be deemed legitimate and hence able for new participants to learn the right method to think, perceive and feel the key themes about members of the organization".

"Here there are decisions decided through an agreement." "Here is where we purchase from the retailer who offers the most competitive rates." "Here is where the men go to work, while women remain in the house." "Here there, the women are independent and live their own decisions." "Nature can be described as an asset that is used by men." "Nature has a sacred value, and man's responsibility is to protect it."Each of these statements demonstrates an idea of culture. Ideas form a mental model that outlines what is the (reality) that is a society.

Inside any organization (families and professions, organisations or industries, nations) collective mental models develop from the experiences of others. Through time the members of the group confront problems. As they respond, they establish the habitual method (in the terms of Bateson) of looking at the situation and taking action. It becomes component of the mental model of the group, and can be passed through generations to form the "knowledge" from the entire group. However, with its retrogression during the dark of night, this knowledge loses its experiential roots and becomes an absolute fact. It is no longer "the way our collective has faced the issues of the past" we now have "the only way to be facing the current challenges and in the future."

Mental models of the collective are an extremely dangerous weapon like individual mental models On other hand, they aid in groups to organize the efficient and efficient implementation of their own reality basing their reality on previous experiences. But, to the contrary, they decide the possible range of future scenarios. Self-validation is a way to ensure peace and stability within groups - and when faced with drastic changesin the culture (which is usually conservative) could turn into a lifesaver for the group. The challenge to beliefs that are shared creates tension and entrapment. The process of changing cultural beliefs is a very difficult process.

Personal Background

The fourth factor that influences mental models is our personal history such as gender, race nationality, ethnicity family, influences from the family, economic and social status as well as the level of education we have received and the way in which we have received treatment from our parentsand siblings and the way we began working and became self-sufficient, and so on. Each of these influences shape the mental model we use to navigate through the world. As the collective experience of learning becomes the basis of a society, personal experiences of learning are stored in the foundational layers of consciousness. They also give us automatic ways to perceive and take action.

There are certain assumptions in the mental model people are taught from the beginning of their years of life, long before they are able to think critically. In the course of their lives, these subconsciously learned beliefs underlie the abyss of opinions, beliefs and actions that people consider "obvious." As an instance the girl was raised in a household that was ruled by an absent father which, in consequence she believes that "men aren't reliable enough to perform their duties." However the son of the same family grows believing that "men can be as they please."

Our history is part of the past but our mental models translate this back into future. As a computer does the brain has continuous access to all the life experiences stored in its memory, and it can apply these experiences to the future and present, as a way to interpret and actions.

This is especially true in the case of mental models that are "anchored" to an unsolved historical event. In these situations it is possible to get caught in a loop that is a symbol of reliving a traumatic incident and trying to alter the outcome. For instance, the person who rages against his boss might be going back to his childhood to settle pending issues in his relationship with father. The indication of the regression is the complete insanity with which the act is executed. In the home seeking to tell his wife the reason why his dismissal the man states, "I do not know the reason why he was fired. When I was told by him to redo the entire work I threw up and yelled towards him. "

Personal experiences and experiences, as well as language and cultural influences create a unique mental model. The mental model can lead a person to identify with certain people and not others; to view things in a particular way and refuse to accept another's ideas; to take certain actions without considering other people; and to determine which actions are acceptable, and what's not. Every person operates according to their own mental model and lives a life that is "his or his" (reality). However, this (reality) could differ from the perception of others who's biology, language and culture, as well as personal stories are distinct. Human beings all share the same world, but perceive it in a different manner. This is the reason why humans do not reside with the same (reality) that is a reality which has grave consequences.

Everyone has mental models that we determine our identity, the way we behave, and also describe our world. There are various types of mental models and they can be capable of guiding a person to either failure or success.

Sometimes your method of thinking and looking at the world can prevent you from taking on the changing and developing as a person and professional. There are some practices that allow thinking models that can be examined and improved to achieve personal development.

Chapter 7: 7 Mental Models That Will Boost Your Productivity Level

The method of looking at the world is distinctive for each person. Most of the time, people is able to see the world with an eye composed of their beliefs opinions, beliefs, prejudices and experiences. But a crystal clear view is never accessible. For instance, if you are looking for the answer to any issue it is your responsibility to determine the most effective solution. Mental models are among the most effective ways to discover the best solution for every kind of problem. It can improve your vision capability by using tested as well as unbiased and tested lenses. In the end, you'll find the right solution that could be beyond your field of expertise. This will give you with an understanding of the world from all over the world. It can also increase your professional standing.

Mental models can help you in different ways. They can help you speed up the process of solving the issue. Mental models aid in understanding the nature of any issue quicker and with greater ease. They can help you discover the most efficient solution. It plays an important role in enhancing the development of both professional and personal. Understanding mental models can help you increase your ability to perceive any thing from the various perspectives. This will improve your flexibility and adaptability within the diverse problem solving areas. Additionally, it will increase your efficiency.

Incentive Programs

Incentives' power lies in hidden forces that influence an individual's behaviour. The idea of incentives is of rewarding individuals with incentives to make them adhere to the commitment of doing something that they would like to do. People will pick the idea based on their own best interests. Charlie Munger explains his favorite illustration from Federal Express related to the incentive power. He believes that incentives are an example of a superpower. He also uses it to describe the reasons why it is possible to take place in every single event throughout human history, regardless of whether it's good or not. If you offer a reward for the population that you provide an incentive to them, they will be motivated to change their behavior.

For instance, Charlie Munger describes in how Federal Express had a dreadful moment when they first started offering overnight shipping. Every night , as all the planes arrived at the central area, employees transferred the parcels between planes as quickly as they could to ensure that the items could be delivered on time. The company discovered that they always arrived in the late hour. The company then implemented the new method and began to pay employees by shift instead of per hour. This meant that workers were able to go home when they finished their shifts. There was no requirement to remain for a long period of time in order to collect more money. If they were able to complete their work in a brief period of time, they could get the same amount. Because of this, many people begun to complete their tasks efficiently, so they could leave early. The planes also left earlier than the time they were scheduled to leave rather than being delayed.

If you're an administrator, you employ incentives to influence the behavior of your team members in the direction you want them to go in. You may offer incentives for your employees to improve their productivity, which is crucial to the development of your company. The assessment of possible adverse consequences is crucial when you decide to offer incentive programs to employees.

There are numerous reasons to suggest that punishment is not the best method to alter an individual's behavior. In general, the power of suppression of punishment could alter behavior. However, it is possible to recur because of the removal of threats to punish. Sometimes, punishment can help consider escape. If escape is not possible, the person becomes more aggressive. In the case of punishment, it can trigger different actions like aggressiveness, escape and helplessness. If you don't perform something, you'll be attempting to learn about the procedure more carefully. The punishment or the negative incentive are not equally effective. If you are looking to tackle your most difficult task, an incentive, such as rewards or penalties is the best method to make it happen quickly. So, any form of reward can increase your efficiency.

Regret Minimization Framework

The regret minimization can be made when you make a choice that provides a feeling of happiness immediately. But , it isn't the best or most efficient. The mental model gives you an understanding of how to assess your choice. It will also help you comprehend how this decision will affect your wellbeing and your success over a long duration. You can determine if your current choice will assist you get a great outcome in the near future by examining the framework of regret minimization. Before making any decision, whether it's small or large it is important to write down your likely regrets.

If you commit a rash decision, you shouldn't make use of the regret minimization framework to justify your actions. It is important to consider the appropriate timing, the current level of expertise, environmental aspects, and various other kinds of forces. You must be flexible when adjusting to different circumstances. It is essential to be focused to reach your goals in your life. The concept of framework for reducing regret will enable you to consider various scenarios and take the decision to say the yes or no option easily. If you're confident that you are following an effective strategy then you are able to make your choice for yes. It is important to be aware of the risks in taking on the risk. You will not regret it if you know your strategy.

You can develop your capacity to comprehend actions that aid to predict behaviour by using the notion of regret. Regret can be described as an emotion that is negative and can be accompanied by cognitive states. It can be a feeling of guilt or sadness. It can also be a feeling of blame for the bad outcome. While regret is cleansing, it can also be a beneficial emotion. Feelings of regret may lead to a corrective action or taking the right path. If regret leads to fewer opportunities and leads to constant stress that is detrimental for your physical body as well as your mind. The pattern of repetitive, negative and self-centered ruminative thoughts is a sign of depression that can lead to mental disorders. It has been proven that chronic stress due stress can trigger an imbalance in hormone production as well as the immune system.

It is important to avoid the possibility of compromises or fear when you begin to do anything to gain a genuine experience or else you'll regret it later. If you have the chance to make a correct choice by making use of the framework for minimizing regret. Try to figure the advantages that can be gained from regret. It is important to think about ways you can better understand yourself. In addition, you should strive to become as a better individual.

Activation Energy

If you're looking to gain an understanding of the energy that activates and the reasons behind the chemical reaction can help. A certain amount of energy is required in order to reach the temperature at which you are trying to ignite an object or ignite a flame. A chemical reaction won't begin until it is stable enough for the product is greater than the stabilities of reaction. If you wish to make burning wood, then the carbon within the wood is transformed into carbon dioxide , which will be more durable than the carbon that is present in the wood. This reaction produces the energy needed to start the process to attain the temperature at which wood ignites serves as the energy needed to initiate the fame or the burning of wood.

You're protected if are aware of the activation energy. If the activation energy has reached a high level, there's the need for more energy input. It is possible to use activation energy to bring about drastic changes to your daily life. If you are looking to take on the next step it is necessary for more energy activation. Psychologists have defined the energy of activation as motivation, and it is crucial to start any endeavor. At times, a person wants to make a drastic and challenging change, such as taking drastic changes to their lifestyle or avoiding an addiction, resigning for a long-term position and avoiding your spouse or loved ones, and other such things. It is vital to reach the point at which is ready to begin the process of breaking. It is necessary to have an enormous amount of activation energy in order to get to the breaking point, or initiate the breaking process.

In chemistry, certain chemical reactions require very high temperatures to create this chemical process. It is also necessary for a very high amount for activation energy. If you'd like to reduce the energy of activation it is necessary to include catalysts. There are two kinds of catalysts. They are catalysts that have positive properties and the negative catalyst. If you wish to complete the reaction in a brief period of time and also make the reaction at a low temperature you'll need the positive catalyst. However when you wish to speed up the process it is best to employ the negative catalyst.

Parkinson's Law

in 1955 Cyril Northcote Parkinson, an economist , wrote "work is expanded to take up the time for completion." It is claimed that doing more work is always better than doing faster and more efficient work. If you are trying to complete something in a brief period of time, you will be creating difficulties and your task will be difficult and intimidating. There isn't enough time to do your research. In addition, you'll experience stress and anxiety to complete your task in the stipulated time. If you allocate the appropriate amount of time for the task, you'll be able to do your research in a sufficient amount of time and the difficulty of the task will decrease. You'll be able finish the task in the specified time. Parkinson's Law offers good results because people have enough time for the task in the context of the task actually requires.

It is possible to apply Parkinson's Law within your work in your daily routine. Your workplace won't an issue or you could apply it at workplace, home or wherever. It can help you attain high-quality performance at work. It will allow you to increase the efficiency of your job. It is necessary to make an inventory of the total quantity of tasks. You will then estimate the amount of time that will be required to finish the task. Following that, you need to determine the amount of time needed to complete each task. It is recommended to set aside half of the time needed to complete each task yourself. It is important to consider this set time frame for each task important as a deadline for all work. It is essential to set a time at the end of your task without taking any type of shortcuts or poor quality output.

Your improvement in effectiveness requires you to test how effectively you keep track of time in accordance with the set timeframe for the job. The setting of the timeframe for your project is among the most effective ways to accomplish your task effectively. There are occasions when you will not be able to complete your work on time, as per the above-mentioned method. It is possible to find a solution by increasing the workload, and it's an unique method of increasing your productivity. If you take on the burden of a large amount and it forces you to perform more work in accordance with the task that you did before. It will be an effort to complete the work on time. If you are able to finish the task faster you're relaxed and don't accept any potential interruption. This is because you are aware of your ample time, and you have the ability to use the time for other uses.

Parkinson's Law is one of the most effective ways to boost your productivity. It can help you stay inspired and energized to complete your work in time. It is helpful to understand the best way to keep the time you spend on tasks from becoming wasted. It is possible to increase efficiency by adjusting your timing and the scope of work you have to complete.

Single Tasking

If you are doing one thing at one time, this is one-tasking. However it is when you are doing multiple tasks simultaneously it is known as multitasking. Multitasking is more difficult and requires you to try to complete more than one task. Due to this, your brain will wander while multitasking and your focus can decrease. Multitasking is the process of completing a lengthy list of tasks, which means lower concentration. It's not great for your health and stems from stress to handle a heavy workloads in a timely manner. In contrast the single-tasking method lets you concentrate and do a lot of research within the subject. If you do it consistently and regularly, it can help to regain or increase the ability to focus your mind and concentrating. If you decide to focus on one task you will be able to enjoy the task due to less stress.

There are numerous benefits of working in a single-task, and the benefits are as the following:

The brain is an essential component in the body of a human. The brain is the control center for all tasks you carry out. The brain uses a significant amount of energy within your body to carry out different kinds of tasks. When you're multitasking, your brain uses lots of energy to constantly shift your mind to accomplish various tasks. In contrast you don't have to try or shift your thinking to accomplish different tasks when working on a single task. This means that less energy is required to complete a single task. It's also helpful to be energetic in order to handle the other work you have to do.

If you conduct research or are involved in a single-tasking activity your thinking capacity will be a major factor. It will allow you to discover all the potential advantages and uses of the task. In the end, as a result your efficiency will improve in the particular field.

The single-tasking process requires your focus to a single thing, and it helps to keep quality work. When you're working on a single task that is, you are focused on the subject you are studying. It can help you increase your efficiency, which plays a an important role in completing the obligations you have made in your personal and professional life.

Through strengthening your ability to concentrate For instance the single-tasking technique helps in preventing your mind from becoming distracted.

If you find yourself engaged in a single task frequently the focus of your focus will expand. You'll be able to complete your job more efficiently and your excellence will result in success quickly.

It is beneficial to multitask to enhance your relationships which play an important role in the daily life. When you're multitasking, you'll try to ignore the phone or responding to questions asked by others. Because of this it will affect your relationships with other people. In the opposite you'll be free from anxiety and stress as you engage in only one task. You will be able to feel peace within your soul. You won't feel any anxiety to answer any phone call or to answer any questions asked by others. This will assist you in enhance your relationships at home or at work.

Pareto's Principle

Pareto's Principle enables you to identify the top performing actions and pinpoint the element that will yield the most effective outcome. It will help you effectively manage your time by applying Pareto's Principle. Additionally, you will be able save time by staying clear of techniques that produce less of returns. Pareto's Principle can be applied by following the steps below:

First, you need be focused on the elements that can yield outcomes. Imagine you create an inventory of 25 things that you'll be focusing on in the near future.

In the next step, you must note the five most important items.

It is recommended to try these techniques and then ignore the rest.

It is a common principle when you complete the chosen five items. Each time, you will create the list completely fresh, including 25 items.

It will allow you to see clearly the what is important to your work.

In 1906 In 1906, in 1906, an Italian economics expert, Vilfredo Pareto observed that the majority of the surface of Italy was occupied from 20% of populace of Italy. He explained that the majority of the result is generated from only 20% efficiency or input. It is also known as the 80/20 rule. In adherence to the Pareto's Principle that you will reap many advantages. These benefits are:

Improved productivity: The application of the 80/20 rule or Pareto's Principle can help you identify the area that you need to focus your time and effort for maximum efficiency. Based on the rule of 80/20, if an employee prioritizes 20percent of most important tasks, they'll get 80percent of the results. It is also recommended in accordance with the Pareto Principle to not be wasting time with some that aren't suitable to provide the long-term benefits. It is also recommended to place importance on certain resources that improve productivity. Pareto Principle also helps to identify the reasons for lower productivity, and also the most effective solutions to the issues that are less productive.

Increased profitability: Regardless the type of business you run it is a typical circumstance in any company that more than 20% of salespeople in a company generate around the majority of sales. Pareto's Principle can help determine whether the importance of the efforts and resources that are 20% of employees that generate a substantial number of sales , allowing for the improvement of their skills or to put priority to the other 80% of salespeople struggling to boost sales within the company.

Optimization of Website: You are able to examine the speed at which the flow of traffic on the page of your site applying the Pareto's Principle. This will assist you in improving the performance of your site making sure that it is easy to browse through or navigate to the most important webpage of your site to the visitors. This will help you increase sales for your business , and also accelerate the growth of your company.

Chapter 8: A Brief A History Mental Models And Influential Figures Which Have Used Them.

The concept of mental models has been around since the 1800s, using mental models to represent the underlying concepts of concepts. If you're more knowledgeable about these mental models you stand more chance of success in solving problems as well as decision-making general. Before we dive into the guidelines you should keep in mind in applying different mental models, let's have a some time to look back at the background of mental models, and how they've been used by some of the most influential individuals in our world in the present.

A Short Review of the History of Mental Models

American Philosopher Charles Sanders Peirce is credited with the first ideas in mental models, which is the mental representation of ideas that are actual, imagined or hypothetical. In a book published in 1896, Peirce explored the idea of reasoning as a kind of model for the mind. Peirce stated that it is an act in which a person "examines the situation that are stated in the premisses and draws diagrams of this situation, and observes in the various parts of the diagram relationships that are not explicitly mentioned in precepts, is satisfied by conducting mental tests on the diagram that these relationships will always exist or at the very least subsist in a certain percentage of instances and then concludes that they are their essential or probable reality."

Other authors also explored the concept using mental representations in their work. Kenneth Craik, a Scottish psychologist said in the book that our brain uses small-scale representations of reality. These bits that represent reality can be used think about events, plan for them, and to find the underlying reasons. Every mental model is created with a structure closely related to the nature of the scenario it is describing. For instance an architect creating models of the size of a structure could be a model mental. an art of visualisation that is created based on the same hypothetical or real construction that it's intended to depict.

Since Craik has been around, other researchers have also discussed the notion of mental models, and how they can be used. A number of cognitive scientists have weigh on the value of mental models that are heavily influenced by the person's perceptions and opinions about an event.

Physical physicist Richard Feynman is another noted for his work using mental models. While he was attempting towards obtaining the Ph.D. at Princeton as well as the undergraduate diploma from MIT He was frequently noticed for his frequent visits to the math department to solve problems, even those that were the Ph.D. pupils were not capable of working on. The secret? Feynman was taught a method in physics class at high school that transformed his life.

After noticing that Feynman moved and talked all the time in class, the teacher talked to him at school after school about the issue. Feynman seemed bored. He then gave Feynman a book to read in class: Advanced Calculus, written by Woods. The teacher instructed him to be at the back of class during class and not speak instead of reading the book until he'd completed the entire book. In that period, Feynman began developing mental models. He learned to utilize an integral sign to create and distinguish parameters. Although the integral method isn't typically used in graduate programs, Feynman had mastered it. He was able to solve these issues not because he was smarter or had more knowledge, but because he was using an entirely different set of tools than the Ph.D. mathematics students. The tools that he used enabled him to look at problems in a different manner and led him to the answer.

Mental Models Throughout History

Historical scholars believe they believe that Renaissance or Enlightenment both represent significant shifts in the belief system of the time. The Renaissance was a period of change that occurred between the 14th to 17TH century. In the preceding centuries, prior to the Renaissance there was a strong emphasis on the religion of Christianity. Things like the Black Death that killed an estimated 75-200 million people in Europe made people feel that God was unjust. There was a more distinct line between state and church, and the beliefs that were prevalent at the time focused more on having fun and exploration of the world. It was at this time that art, writing philosophy, art, and sciences gained popularity as people searched for a better understanding.

The Enlightenment period also revealed an evolution in the attitudes of society and beliefs that could be described as a change in mental model. The Enlightenment period was a time of greater acceptance of the notion that human beings are subject to universal physical laws and do not be a creature created by a divine being. Discovering physical law led to new concepts possible, including mass production technology as well as changes in the structure of economics. This made it possible for people to look at their world in fresh ways, expanding their mental models and permitting an extensive exploration of areas such as engineering, math and sciences.

Influential Persons Who've Employed Mental Models

Many of the people who have made it to the top, such as Jeff Bezos, Warren Buffett, Charlie Munger, and Elon Musk, have attributed some of their achievement to their capacity to think and to learn.

Warren Buffett, Charlie Munger, and Mental Models

Warren Buffett is well-known for his expertise as an investor however the business partnership he shares with Charlie Munger is given less recognition. Munger is somewhat out of the spotlight of finance, but is well-known for his long-running work making mental models. The most renowned speeches on mental models was delivered by Charlie Munger at USC Business School in 1994. While the intention was to address his philosophy of business and investment strategies, he presented a general model for making smart decisions. It's this kind of decision making that separates the difference between success and failure. Business partners Warren Buffett had also used these mental models that allowed both of them to develop into learners. They were able to tackle problems from various perspectives prior to deciding on an option, which helped they to come to the best and most successful business choices. The models employed by business leaders such as Buffett or Munger are guidelines that provide a reasoned conclusion that is accepted by the vast majority of people. So, any data that is able to be put into a particular mental model can be examine it from a specific perspective. With the various mental models available to analyse any issue it is possible to reduce the degree of uncertainty in their lives and be certain that the decisions they make are ones which will yield the most beneficial outcome.

In a sense mental models can help a person become more intelligent. This isn't just an accumulation of information or concepts, but rather the method by which ideas and knowledge are utilized in the process of making decisions. Many people ignore the complexity in the world around them and do not realize how much impact it affects their lives. Most people are focused on a handful of things and the results they can expect to achieve. However there are millions of variables that impact one single scenario. The results are seen as surface-level due to the fact that they don't consider these additional variables. The solution isn't to take into account all of those variables. It is so numerous factors that could affect a situation that it's difficult to determine which factors to concentrate on to influence the outcome in as you would like. In addition, it's impossible to control every factor that is involved in a particular situation. Instead of overwhelming your brain with all these small details, many people use mental models. While there isn't a one perfect model, it is important to remember that perfection isn't required for the mental model to be effective. They're merely tools that can make the many variables that make the decision easier to consider.

According to Munger the importance is to seek proficiency in mental models in a variety of disciplines. Some of the fields Munger has been studying and acquiring the foundations of include physics, accounting as well as psychology, finance architecture, economics, medicine mathematics as well as geography, history as well as sociology, biology and the chemistry. The rationale behind the idea is because there exist aspects in every discipline that help to build a set of cognitive models. Although everyone agrees that there are cognitive models more useful than others, and more adaptable to real life situations, but not all mental models are available inside the same discipline. Mental models used by people are typically incorrect because they focus on one particular area. For instance, businesspeople take decisions based on certain guidelines they apply to weigh the benefits and risks. A researcher or scientist could use theories or research to resolve issues. This isn't necessarily a negative thing; however, it hinders an individual's ability to perceive the entire range of possibilities when it comes to problem-solving and making decisions.

Another thing to bear on your mind is the fact that similar mental models will not apply to every person. It is almost impossible to master the dozens of fields to the level necessary to master certain of the more complicated mental models. Luckily, the most effective models are that are based on simplicity, not complex concepts. It is not necessary to know the subject matter to understand the fundamental principles. A basic understanding of different disciplines can help you look at problems and make decisions from different angles, providing you more possibilities and a greater likelihood of being successful.

As you discover the various mental models It is important to choose the most effective. Certain mental models can be employed to build the framework for your own work however others can be utilized just by being aware of the existence of.

Musk and Mental Models. Musk as well as Mental Models

Many believe that Elon Musk's record of achievements to be incredible. Even though he's in his mid-40s, he has four companies that have been successful that specialize in transportation, software, energy and aerospace. Many credit this amazing achievement to his working hours of more than 80 hours as well as his goal-setting and determination But, not all possess these qualities, but they're not enough to take his company to the exact success. One thing Musk does possess that others aren't is his ability to comprehend a variety of disciplines. Musk has been able to master many fields throughout his life, including subjects like rocket engineering, science, physics construction, artificial Intelligence, construction solar power, and energy.

One of the main reasons Elon Musk is capable of dedicating the time and energy required to achieve his success in general is that the fact that he is an apex polymath. This is a term used to describe people who have a wide range of knowledge in various fields for an average of five hours a week. If they are able to learn about every one of these disciplines they are able to comprehend the more fundamental theories as well as mental model that link the various disciplines. As more and more mental models are accumulated, they can be used to the chosen area of expertise.

What we can learn from polymaths such as Elon Musk is that there is value in learning multiple fields. One of the most famous sayings is, "Jack of all trades master of none." If you examine the many polymaths who have made it big nowadays it's clear that this is not the case. They benefit due to their knowledge of many different areas, such as:

A world-class skill set developed by combining skills that are not typical

Gaining advantage from information

Increased chances of success in your career

A better perspective across different areas

The separation from global economics

When you are specialized in multiple fields there's a resemblance of ideas you can develop. For instance, a person working in the technology business who is knowledgeable about biology could use this knowledge to develop innovative concepts. According Musk Musk the key to success in a variety of disciplines is to study them, and then using what's known as transfer of learning.

Learning transfer refers to the process of learning in one field and applying it to anotherarea, whether in practical or an sector. When these basic concepts are merged, it offers an array of decisions and strategies for problem solving.

One of Musk's numerous methods is taking mental models and concepts from the subject matter he's acquired. Instead of being focused on a single concept or factual information, it is divided into more manageable components.

To break this information into fundamental principles It is recommended to have other fundamental principles to compare it with. This is the primary benefit of a multidisciplinary approach. If the same case is studied, it's almost impossible to dissect the data into a manner that can be managed. Through examining diverse cases from different disciplines, the facts and fundamental concepts become more clear. It's also easier to grasp the connections between different parts of the information.

Let's look at how Elon Musk uses this. The fields Elon Musk has learned the fundamental theories of are technology artificial intelligence, physics and engineering. Then, these concepts were utilized to create new ideas such as autonomous vehicles Tesla as well as SpaceX. The most effective way to evaluate these concepts is to reflect on the things each principle is reminiscent of. Instead of focusing on the subject you're studying, consider how it could be applied to other areas that you know about. Next, think about what it is that you are reminded of about this topic and draw connections.

Jeff Bezos and Mental Models

Prior to when Jeff Bezos started Amazon, He employed the framework of regret minimization of thinking. Bezos thought of a brilliant idea, but was not quite ready to make the leap and start Amazon. The initial plan was to establish an online shop that would sell books. Every person he spoke to believed it was a good idea, but his boss put it on the side. In the end, Bezos already had a lucrative, well-paying job. So what did he gain by making the leap?

The framework for minimizing regret plays a role because it offered Bezos the ability to imagine the possibilities of the concept. He only had 48 hours in making the decision that would alter his life. The best way to minimize regret is simple. Consider, "Will I regret not doing this after some time?" If Bezos had not brought his idea to fruition, then he would have created Amazon the company that would continue to grow exponentially after its inception.

For you to effectively utilize this model, you need to imagine the future, and then take a look back. If you don't expect to regret doing something then don't spend your time and energy into it. If you are at risk of regret, it's best to carry out the plan and turn it into the realisation. Bezos said:

"I believed that when I reached the age of 80 I wouldn't regret trying this. I wasn't going regret taking part in this new thing known as the Internet I believed would be an enormous deal. I knew that if did fail, I wouldn't be regretting my decision, yet I also knew that the only thing I could regret is not trying."

The main benefit of regret reduction you discern is that it prompts you to move forward and think beyond the present. If you take a look back from the future it allows you to evaluate the situation from a different angle. This allows for a more accurate analysis of the decision as well as the possible results.

How to Make Use of Mental Models to Transform Your Life

You can clearly see that many of the most successful and influential people around the globe are based on models of mentality. Buffett as well as Munger are well-known for making use of the mental model to come up with sound investment decisions, analyzing possible investments for indicators that they are likely to experience rapid growth. Elon

Musk is a researcher of mental models and the fundamentals across a variety of disciplines, using his extensive expertise to develop new concepts. And, of course, Jeff Bezos has used mental models to make his decisions which helped him to start a hugely successful business.

Although all of them are extremely hardworking They are always gathering information and sorting it out using the many mental models available to them. By using the same strategies and methods, you can too start changing the way you think about reality.

The truth is that the universe is built on causality and effect. Even if you do not have a clear idea of the consequences of your choice It is your choices which set the stage. In the event that Jeff Bezos had never decided to take the risk and create the company or even if someone else had started Amazon or his own life might have been quite different.

Similar is the case when it comes to solving problems. In solving issues, you're restricted to the possibilities you have in your mind. It is not possible to solve a problem using an answer that you've thought of but haven't yet. If you are able to understand the fundamentals of different disciplines, you will have an array of options that you can employ to solve your problems. This will give you the most effective results. When your decision-making and problem-solving abilities improve, you'll eventually be able to decide on the life you'd like and start living it. Everything is feasible.

The construction of an Latticework Of Mental Models

It's not enough to keep a record of pages of models in your mind and hope that they remain in place. It is much better to focus on mastering a specific discipline at each time. Pick a subject and then explore the fundamentals, then focus on that particular discipline and its principles until you grasp its basic latticework and how it connects to other ideas you've been studying. As per Charlie Munger:

"You need to master all the major concepts in the major disciplines in such the way that they form a mental latticework inside your head , and you will immediately apply them to the remainder in your lifetime."

One way to think of developing mental models is to imagine an actual house. Before you begin making mental models and understanding the ways they are connected to other areas you've been studying, you'll require the foundation to be solid. After that, you'll create the foundation and plug into electrical wiring and plumbing. As with a home it is important for that your models of mentality to be built well and something you'll make use of for many the years to in the future. Alongside studying the different disciplines, it's important to link the ideas together in a manner that allows them to be more effective in conjunction than on their own.

Chapter 9: The Art Of Creative Thinking

People who are creative are 'crazy because they challenge the standard, and are unaffected by the absurd and the bizarre.

They love to twirl with the unusual and the bizarre, as well as the unusual. Every leap forward and improvement that mankind has made is the result of the creativity of some of the most brilliant minds.

It is possible to master all guidelines of the fundamentals and rational reasoning of logic but it will not assist. The pursuit of knowledge, the search for truth and the wisdom of everyday life are a long way from the realm of logic or rationality as life is rapid and constantly changing, and is laced with shocks and surprises. The challenges of life can't often be solved with standard solutions; they require a fresh evaluation.

Creativity requires the ability to think of ideas and imagine things that go beyond the realm of logic and rationality. In popular languages this is described as 'thinking outside the box"!

This is what imagination is all about: choosing the new route that no one has taken before!

Creativity will come from the liberation of intellectual deprivation free from the chains of conservatism and traditional dogmatism.

It's unimaginable for anyone who is creative who keeps himself inside the chambers of dogmatic intellectualism and encases himself within the confines of philosophical theories. Innovative thinkers have certain characteristics that they share They don't hesitate to explore new realms;

They are not afraid to play with related fields of study They are enthusiastically taking excursions into unexplored fields of study. If it's true the idea of imagination is not for those who lack the resources to pursuit of innovation.

We are often held by the notion that imagination is primarily about inventing something that is truly novel and innovative which, in turn, is the prerogative of gifted individuals. It's a false assumption!

In reality, the term "imagination" refers to be the ability to connect unrelated concepts in an extraordinary way. It is a unique imagination that comes by the fusion of diverse ideas concepts, thoughts, or thoughts.

Linear thinking is different from intersectional thinking

Because proper training is designed to improve the foundations of specific disciplines, diligently shaping the brain to conform to the model of linearity.

In simple terms, linearity is one-dimensional thinking! It requires the brain to investigate the language of logic and reasoning. It also robs it of simultaneously the capacity to think out of the norm. This is, in turn, an exercise to master the mundane and monotonous, causing predictable shifts in the process.

Linear thinking is not capable of creating radical change since it encloses the circle within which it conducts its journey of the process of learning. It cannot leave the group, as it content its needs by making small changes here and small changes small there, with no interruption to the current status quo.

The vast majority of the latest innovations triggered by linear thinking are of this type: policy adjustments and procedure changes, as well as structural modifications are all part of the class of linear thinking. These aren't life-altering or transformative changes but are incremental ones.

Intersectional thinking, on contrary, is a technique that takes unpredictability that can, in the end, can alter the environment dramatically. Intersectional thinking is unhindered and cuts across various disciplines and domains to create connections between seemingly not related concepts and ideas. it generates cutting-edge concepts and concepts.

There are many examples of intersectional thinking and include Steve Jobs making the appearance that he observed through the program in calligraphy or applying that knowledge to iPads, iPods, iMacs or iPhones;

It is Alexander Graham Bell who had combined his interests in ventriloquism, auto mechanics, music therapy, and speech therapy to develop the telephone or Leonardo da Vinci that drew his wealth of ideas and information from various disciplines such as engineering and architecture, painting, geology, sculpting, and anatomy, they all point to the capability of these men to link two seemingly unrelated subjects to create a unique result.

In general, interconnected thinking requires an open mind to connect theories and concepts of one field with the concepts and principles from someone other discipline.

Whatever it is related to food recipes or academic research or telecom networks, linking disparate concepts is an attractive thing as a whole that is in the heart of imagination. Intersectional thinking isn't a problem because its key ingredient is the interlocking and linking of diverse ideas and creating the creation of a synergy.

Creative thinking is a process that cannot be bought or manufactured or faked. Neither can it be taught through books, though it could be developed with some adjustment to our perception. The blocks to creativity reside inside the brain and act as blocks to conceptualization hindering the ability to think of different ideas and ways to solve challenges and constraints.

Each and every person is flooded with more sensations than we are able to be able to handle. As you read this, you probably do not know the location that is your vision, sound of your body, or the color of your clothing that are affixed to your body.

Even though all the information is provided in this article, you're probably not aware of anything until you actually observed your thoughts.

Naturally, we don't have time to consider the endless stream of information that are fighting to grab our focus. If we did, it would lead us to information overload and make us a mess.

So, we take out signals that aren't suitable and only focus on those we think are helpful for the purpose. This specific focus is not only beneficial, but also it also blocks vital and comforting signals that are likely to provide life-changing information.

The right training has taught us to see the language of logic and reason. The fascination with 'right answers' has always had precedence over 'imagination' in the workplace.

The fascination with the best way of doing things valued over 'innovativeness.' This has resulted in slowing down of improvisation and experimentation and stifling imagination in the process.

Imaginery is usually afflicted because of four weaknesses: constancy complacency, compression, as well as dedication.

Constancy: An universal notion is given to us that consistency in thought or word is an attribute. Any one with a unique low inconstancy could be considered not trustworthy, undesirable, or insecure.

In the business world, the principal characteristic of command techniques is to limit deviations from the normal. Invariably, the concept of constant change can be brought to a certain spiritual state within the regular plan of things.

However, when you look closer it is apparent that the same vigor, which tries to achieve anticipated outcomes, smudges beneath the spark of imagination, striving to unleash its imaginative expression.

Many people, when faced with the issue, fight it based on past experiences or seek precedent in resolving the issue. They are convinced that they should be thinking to think vertically! They believe in the vertical!

A vertical focus implies that the narrow view is delineating the problem in one way instead of understanding it in many different ways. Anyone who is driven by a belief that it isn't worthwhile to look at multiple options is bound to fall by the creative process.

The problem with constancy is when one is forced to submit the issue to a personal interpretation.

A problem, for instance, can be identified and evaluated using a variety of possibilities of interpretations: using symbolic or non-verbal interpretations mathematically or numerically through the use of sensory images like scent, taste touching, and seeing through thoughts and emotions like anger, excitement and hatred, or by using obvious images like mental maps.

The more varied the understanding of an issue.The more likely are the risk of developing new outcomes.

Constancy is a hindrance to creativity. Constancy is nothing more than a recurrence of similarity and the sameness

A third virtue that can be a hindrance to imagination is commitment. It causes the creative juices to stop especially when we identify issues based on previous experiences.

The general human tendency is to view the current problems as variations on previous events; therefore we come up with solutions similar to those who were successful in earlier times, totally unaware of the fact that things are being seen differently and being interpreted differently. The desire to remember the past allows us to tackle issues in a stereotypical way, and not to think creatively.

The commitment to a certain viewpoint can also hinder discovering commonalities across diverse issues. It is also difficult to see a common approach that solves multiple issues at the same time.

Looking at disparate parts holistically is the hallmark of creative thinkers. Ray Kroc, the male who was the driving force behind the creation of McDonald's was not the first to come up with the idea of fast food. He worked as a salesman before the concept was reconstructed by something completely different.

Connecting a standard menu, even food preparation methods and consistent quality of service and hygiene of facilities as well as affordable food production and food waste materials and combining them with his sales expertise as well as his entrepreneurial spirit and relationship-building skills, he showed an innovative method of thinking.

Each and every one of the features mentioned above is unique, however the founder incorporated them all to create the concept which, even to this day, has proven to be a financially viable and sustainable business model.

Compression: A lot of information and duplicate data is enough to drive anyone insane. Time pressure, stress and the lack of resources hinder our capacity to investigate the problem thoroughly. As a result we present numerous details. We place artificial constraints on us when dealing with problems.

We draw boundaries, sit in them, and dream ideas for solutions to our problems. There's a reluctance due to impersonal factors or personal preference to think creatively when solving problems. People often are prone to making assumptions without understanding their assumptions and examining alternatives to find hidden clues.

Compression erodes the capacity to separate between the grain from the dust. It also reduces the capability to eliminate inaccurate or inaccurate information that is not relevant. Indecisive minds combine a variety of information into a jumbled collection and are then burdened by the weight of it. This complicates the problem while edging against the simplicity of problem definition.

It is mental lazyness! It's the result of insufficient interest and aversion to mental work. Lack of willingness to ask questions the inability to focus on studies and fear about the shame of showing one's ignorance are a few reasons that people start to become less interested. Two factors are vital in this case first) an eagerness to ask questions , and the second) the desire to find solutions.

Beat mental inertia! Imagine occurs when you are with the right part of your brain which is focused on the ability to synthesize, intuition and having fun. Our highly well-organized training and structured tasks often emphasis on using more of the left side of our brain, which is responsible for reasoning, stream of consciousness and analytical jobs, with its counterpart, which is situated at the exact opposite end.

Make use of both sides of your mind to be imaginative. As the right brain is helpful in the development of new ideas the left hemisphere assists by processing and understanding them by the process of logical analysis.

Today, competition is a reality that comes from every corner, nook and direction of the universe. The greatest competitive advantage lies not in the gap in income as well as the entitlement gap, gaps in education, or the abilities gap, but rather on the gap in imagination. It is often the case that creativity will be the key to deciding the difference between the haves and the not-so-haves in the modern world.

Systems Thinking Basic Concept

Systems thinking as utilized today has been in use for about sixty years, although it has enjoyed an enviable market share among nonscientists in the last 10 years or thereabouts.

Systems thinking is a more effective approach to look at individuals, events as well as entities throughout the world. It does not consist of two strict methods and theories. It is an assortment of concepts and practices that give methods thinkers a different and possibly more expansive perspective on the world.

In a way, the methods aren't existent within the world but instead depend on human observers seeing things and entities in systems. But, seeing things on the planet as methods can be a very effective way to comprehend their behaviour.

Systems thinkers generally view things as collection of regular interactions as well as processes and shifts. In a sense, systems are a wonderful and essential alternative to the positive perspective that conventional reductionist science.

Self-described methods thinkers have an extensive literature base that is both scientific and non-scientific. The foundation is comprised of methods theories philosophical concepts, philosophies, and methodology.

Systems thinking can be applied into nearly any area which we want to know betterabout, including machines, businesses and social institutions as well as the human brain and computers.

Let me share the four most common methods of thinking that will give you an idea of how methods think about is a rough estimate.

System environment boundaries: Looking at the numerous elements and processes that exist in the globe as methods need and a line between the device at issue and its surrounding.

In the case of example, if would like to envision the family unit as an entity, the boundaries that we draw could divide members of the household from schools or workplaces, as well as communities where they regularly participate.

If we would like to see the cell as a method, then the border could be the cell's wall. Keep in mind that the surroundings of a method could be, if viewed from a different viewpoint, represent other approaches. The boundaries between systems and environments can be physical or conceptual.

2. Closed versus open methods Certain systems are essentially closed, which means that they reduce the impact their

environment exerts on processes. Open systems, in contrast, can change dramatically in response to the inputs of their environments.

For example, a small business is much more open than an automobile engine that is constantly changing to stay afloat however the motor must remain the same as long as it's functioning effectively.

3. Self-contained: One of the characteristics of self-contained systems is that the majority of the procedures and the elements needed to perform their different duties are within their systems.

In reality, every method consumes a variety of sources of energy from earth (or other methods) and then transform those inputs in outputs. However, healthy methods are able to perform their tasks (based on green inputs and sending outputs to the surrounding environment) in a way that is self-contained.

4. Adaptive: Certain devices with higher level of complexity, such as biological organisms and social systems can adapt to constantly changing environment conditions.

Simply put, no matter whether you believe that the environment is changing in the course of time (i.e. macro weather patterns, types of food readily available, changes in other community systems such as.) They are generally adept at adapting to change, improve itwork, and thrive in these changing conditions.

While the concept of methods thinking hadn't yet begun to develop at the at the time of the quote It is evident that Einstein was aware of systems thinking, even though Einstein did not explicitly mention the same. He understood that if we approached problems using the same approach and approach them the same way, we'll continue to achieve the same outcomes.

Humans tend to be creatures of habit and often we think it's difficult to recognize behaviors which are not productive. Systems thinking offers methods and procedures that allow organisations to identify patterns and connections that lead to higher efficiency.

Methods thinking was born out of the discipline of systems dynamics. it's both a set of tools and a innovative method of thinking that uses the use of a brand new language.

Systems thinking is when we think about the whole system rather than trying to reduce it down to the individual parts. That is, we are able to expand our thinking, instead of being reductionist.

When we view of the whole and the entire picture, we're more efficient in identifying patterns and connections over time. Also, we can see that the problem may be indicative of more serious issues within the device and therefore we start looking for the root cause. When we do this we shift our blame and focus to the results we want to see.

Systems thinking is both circular and proactive rather than linear thinking which tends to react. Three fundamental concepts in methods of thinking. strengthening feedback, balancing response, and delays. The reinforcement or amplifying of feedback loops is what propels growth or lead to a decrease of the methods.

They typically spiral upwards or down, but they rarely occur on their own. There are restrictions both to growth and decline. An example of the reinforcing loop is the way that an organization's efficiency could impact development. This, can in turn influence the financial incentives that come full circle and impact the effectiveness. This loop could take a straight direction or an incorrect one but it will eventually come to an upper limit.

Feedback loops that balance or stabilize are those that attempt to keep equilibrium. They are goal-oriented and are able to perform whatever is necessary to achieve or keep that goal. The previous illustration of driving a car is a balancing circuit since the goal is to get to the desired location.

A driver is going to do whatever is necessary to reach the destination safely and efficiently. In the workplace, we're moving up and down the balancing circle when there is an attempt to get the change to take us back to where we started.

There is a resistance to change since the present product is trying to maintain a particular objective. However, the goal may not be obvious or even obvious. We may must discover the mental processes that keep this system operating before we can even have a possibility of altering it.

The presence of delays is inevitable in every program, but they are rarely identified. They can lead to instability of processes and the arduous effort to address delays can cause businesses being either over or under-performing.

What are the characteristics of Methods Thinkers?

Systems thinkers are one who:

Views the whole view.

Modifications to perspectives to identify new areas of leverage within complex systems.

Searches for interdependencies.

It describes how mental models form our futures.

Be aware of the long time.

"Goes to the wide" to think about the complex effects and causal connections.

Unexpected consequences occur.

Lowers"water line "water lines" to focus on the structure and not on blame.

Keeps the tension of paradox and controversy without trying to solve it effectively.

Systems thinkers are those who think outside the box. They are aware that there are no one right answer, and there are many ways to achieve similar outcomes. They realize that quick fixes are likely to result in a return to where they came from and learn to be patient with the idea that cause and effects aren't closely related in time and space.

They know that things can become worse before they improve, however, they've developed the ability to see the long-term perspective. By doing this, they will be able to make use of the synergy and creativity that exists within their organizations.

Chapter 10: Critical Mental Models For Greening

Everyone has mental models that provide our basis to understand and interpret experiences and systems that surround us. Mental models are the thought tools we employ when thinking when making decisions. Mental models influence our behaviour and actions through shaping our thinking processes as well as our perception of systems as well as the world as a whole.

Mental models are a powerful tool which help to organize intricate concepts into a manner that allows us to comprehend and comprehend complex systems. It helps us solve problems, find opportunities, develop ideas, and make informed decisions. The process of filtering information using mental models allows us to gain a better understanding of the system and how it functions.

Mental models are created by our experiences, perceptions, as well as the acquired knowledge which is acquired through the process of learning. Mental models are generally described as:

Mental models are constantly evolving and continually evolving with time and knowledge acquisition

Mental models are merely representations of reality, based on the individual's perception.

Mental models offer simplified explanations of complicated phenomenon

Mind models constitute the fundamental mental models that are the basis of cognition.

Thinking and reasoning are dependent on the mental models are available to us. If we have more models of mentality that we have to help us think and thinking, the greater the variety of occurrences and systems we can be able to comprehend. If we confine our understanding to a narrow range of mental models within our areas that we are experts in, then will develop the tendency to behave and behave according to the same patterns. This results in a decrease in our capacity to be innovative adapting and tackling new challenges are diminished.

Mental models that facilitate simulations of various scenarios within the mind help us predict the possible outcomes of our decisions and actions. The predictive capabilities of mental models can be an important aspect of making decisions and determining what route is most likely to lead us to where we want to go with regard to our goals.

Mental models are well-organized structure in our long-term memory. They are a way to organize various types of information derived from our experiences as well as information that we have learned. They also contain information that is declarative such like names, identities and as well as causal information about how elements of a system work together, and procedural details about how to run a specific system to attain the desired results.

It is the storage and retention of information and other information within our mental models implies that, when we are learning a process like driving or cycling this knowledge is stored in memory, and we can access it at any time to use the specific skill.

Mental model structures are usually constructed as frameworks that are layers of data and pieces of information and concepts which form a bigger system. Its structure is the basis for behavior to be developed. The mental models can be predictive and produce simulations that result from the fundamental information and the knowledge that is inside its structure. Simulations can provide possibilities of outcomes based upon potential scenarios.

Research has demonstrated that knowledge that is organized is more easily remembered and use, so mental models can aid in the recollection of information as well as the development of skills based on the basis of procedural knowledge.

The process of creating the mental model typically takes place in three distinct phases:

Identifying the parts of the system.

Inter intergrating the parts of the system on their interactions

Test and run the model.

The development of mental models and the levels of complexity are dependent on the amount of the experience an individual has. For highly experienced people have a high degree of interconnections between the networks that compose this mental model. Subnetworks are also prevalent in experienced individuals' mental models. The degree of abstraction in these mental models is more complex when associations are present and the idea is built on abstract data rather than on superficial features, which is common for those who are amateurs or have no knowledge.

For those with greater time, subnetworks of information knowledge, information, and concepts typically are built on routinely utilized procedures. They are saved in the mind's model of procedural information. In experienced people, the language is characterized by associations that are based upon understanding the significance of terms within the context that the systems operate in.

The mental model structure in people who are not professionals or with little experience is different from the structures found in brain models used by experts or experienced people. The mental models of amateurs are less sophisticated in terms of abstraction, with concepts built on the surface of things instead of abstract concepts.

Common mental models for amateurs are less interconnected between concepts. The models' networks are not as extensive as the ones in the models of professionals. The language used is an important difference between the structure of both types model mental. For the amateur the word's meaning is determined by natural language , rather than the specific language of the system at hand. The mental model is not a formal one. concepts aren't arranged in a sequential format, as those mental models used by people who have more years of experience.

Expanding your Mental Models

Based on our field of expertise or areas of expertise, we are inclined to develop models that are enriched in one particular field but not so in other fields. The most important factor in achieving excellence in thinking is the development of inter-disciplinary mental models with many and diverse applications as well as applications in various spheres of our lives.

Understanding the fundamental models of the major disciplines like Biology, Physics or commerce will help you be able to comprehend the systems you are studying. Our ideas, beliefs and beliefs are deeply rooted within our minds. We form assumptions and draw assumptions without ever really considering the implications on a conscious or conscious level.

The most effective way to control our thoughts is to first become aware of the thoughts that are influencing us. When you are able to identify the patterns of thought and beliefs that rule your daily life, you are able to try to alter your perspective. We can change our perception of the world by looking at our beliefs that are deeply held and seeking ways to develop, dismantle or even eliminate them based on the effect they have on our perception of reality.

We can create new patterns of thought by:

Find evidence to challenge your assumptions and beliefs, and challenges your assumptions and beliefs.

Our beliefs deeply rooted in our lives are influenced by our emotions as well as past experiences as well as preconceived notions and even our own reasoning. It's therefore hard to change our beliefs as they are deeply ingrained in our lives and, in a significant way define our identity as individuals.

To unravel our deep-seated beliefs, we need to look for proof that they aren't always true. If your view of something is set in a particular manner, you will be limited to seeing facts that support and correspond to your preconceptions. This can cause an inability to evaluate circumstances, and ultimately leads to poor judgment due to the benefit of knowing all the information.

To discredit our convictions, we don't have to prove all of them. Because the majority belief systems are connected by chains that connect one belief system to the next and proving one belief could break the chain and open the door to challenging and discrediting our assumptions. For example, a central belief that you're not smart is linked to a belief that says you can only perform tasks that don't require a superior cognitive ability. By denying the first one, you will instantly eliminate the mental limitations you've placed on your abilities.

A step-by-step method of changing our beliefs systems is the best method to achieve this. When you dissect your beliefs based on idea it becomes easier to alter our mentality. Concepts and beliefs that are ingrained in our minds are often interconnected and breaking the link can unravel the underlying beliefs of our beliefs and force us to create new ones.

Make use of new mental models that expand your perspective

Similar to the as how comfort breeds familiarity the patterns of our thought and mental models provide us a familiar environment that we can operate from. Within our comfort zone, we behave and think similarly, but without stepping outside of the norms we're familiar with.

A mental prison that restricts our cognitive capabilities to a specific patterns is as strict as a physical one. If you are able to only view things in one way, your actions events, experiences, and conclusions will likely remain identical, creating a pattern of predictable choices which will produce the same results which are typical of your choices.

Being open to new possibilities and experiences will require you to adopt new methods of thinking and understanding things. The ability to develop new mental models won't just improve your understanding of systems and the world at large but increase your understanding of the world around you. Multiple mental models offer diverse perspectives from which to comprehend and interpret occurrences and systems.

Understanding better circumstances will improve your decision-making abilities, which will result in better results. By establishing a solid mental model that we can improve our decision-making abilities and improve our capacity to resolve problems and find opportunities.

The accumulation of mental models and the creation of an interconnected network of models helps us improve the capacity to think and the ability to look at things from multiple angles. When we depend on a predetermined number of or a set of mental model, it can restrict our thinking as well as our ability to develop new ideas , and our ability to find solutions to issues.

To make a difference in our lives through behavior changes, we must first alter the way in which we think as well as how our thoughts impact our actions. This can only be achieved by deciding to develop our own set of mental models, and then set aside our preconceived notions. Our attitudes, values beliefs as well as our actions and behaviour are shaped by the thoughts we have. To accomplish anything, we have to first imagine it in our minds before we can turn it to life.

The significance of mental models can be under-emphasized. They not only affect the development of our individual lives However, they also impact the way we interact with others , as well as our performance at work and in other pursuits of knowledge. Thinking about the world from the lens of a single specific subject or body of knowledge can result in a limited and biased view of the world. It also limits the ability of our thinking to reflect the reality.

Our education system concentrates on forming experts in particular fields of study like biology geology, physics, and a myriad of other specialties. To be exceptional thinkers, we have to be prepared to break out from the confines of our areas of expertise and explore the world of liquid knowledge. Liquid knowledge refers to knowledge that is a cross-section of different fields and can be useful throughout every day life.

Liquid knowledge assists in the development of interconnected concepts within the mind model. It creates co-relations between concepts that are related, establishing commonalities and interconnections across various fields of expertise and knowledge. These connections in our mental models are vital to create opportunities and inventing new concepts that could be missed if we restricted our focus to a single field of knowledge.

Understanding the fundamentals of every discipline will broaden your worldview and allow you to see the world from different perspectives and increase your understanding of our world.

adopting new mental Models that are applicable to Business and Organizations

Businesses can also gain from the creation and development sharing mental models. The shared mental models can help to establish organizational cultures that are founded on a common understanding of the company's goals and the course of the actions needed to get the business to its goals.

Sharing mental models is essential in improving efficiency of an organization since they provide a common understanding of the tasks to be completed, encourage collaboration and establish an established system to take decisions and resolve issues.

If companies set common goals as well as a shared vision and motivations for their teams, they can create an atmosphere of cooperation. Within a team-oriented work environment, employees are able to integrate their individual tasks into functional units, where various tasks are carried out, but their overall goal remains the same.

Mental models encourage collaboration by fostering the impression of a common mentality and of thinking. The shared mental models can result in changes in behavior as a result of the culture of an organization that is generated by the adoption the shared mental model.

Mental models like DRI (directly accountable individual) are utilized by successful companies such as Apple to instill an atmosphere of accountability and accountability within the group.

Businesses use mental models that establish clear roles and responsibilities for their employees within their organizations. This is what ensures the effectiveness and efficiency of the business. The shared mental models can allow a company to have efficient leadership and group management tools. In any company individuals from diverse backgrounds meet and must figure out an effective way to function as a group. Each of us has our personal personalities, with distinct beliefs that guide our behavior and actions.

To limit the impact of personal beliefs on work behaviors The mental models that are shared are used to establish a collective mindset and the thinking process that generates common goals, objectives and behaviour. Mental models in an organisation can be used to explain, define and predict the behaviour of teams. It is impossible to have individuals with identical mental models.

However, it is possible that their mental models be compatible in the context of the major perceptions they have and also their systems of processing information and knowledge.

The identification and development of mutually compatible models between team members is the most important goal in creating mental models that are shared by all team members. Being able to create mental models that are compatible signifies that team members share an knowledge of the way in which the task ahead is to be completed and their respective duties in the completion of the mission, and how they can link their roles and responsibilities to form a cohesive team.

Stability and consistency of knowledge is a key component in the framework of shared mental models. Understanding the roles of each member of the team will allow for an explicit plan of actions based on the defined duties of each member and what each team member must be doing to support each other's activities.

The workforces that require a higher degree of coordination to operate efficiently such as firefighters and paramedics are dependent on common mental models that unite the individual roles in an effective way that team effectiveness can be enhanced. When emergency responders are called in an emergency understanding the role of each member in the team helps to ensure there aren't gaps in their response protocols and, in turn, assist in determining where to most effectively position each member of the response team in order to increase the efficiency and effectiveness of the group.

Insufficient understanding of roles and functions leads to confusion regarding the objectives of the business and what is expected from employees within the organization. When the roles and specific duties are not clearly defined this can lead to the duplication of duties or aspects of the task not being completed because team members lack specific information regarding their roles and their respective roles.

Effective teams make use of shared mental models in order to forecast and simulate possible outcomes by using various scenarios. The predictive nature in mental models can be vital in identifying potential obstacles which could affect the accomplishment of goals, and determining the best way to overcome these challenges. The ability to forecast the future will assist the company plan and planning to prepare for future events. A capacity to identify challenges and spot weak points ensures that team members can collaborate and work together in various situations to increase their effectiveness as a team.

The shared mental models are essential to creating the cohesion of workplaces through

A mutual understanding of the roles and the functions needed to accomplish an assignment or meet the objectives of the company.

Implementing effective communication systems and processes between team members.

Establish a sense of the individuals' roles and the role of each within the group and the ways in which these roles interplay in order to help complete the project.

Facilitate anticipation of team demands and predict possible results

Find common goals and a purpose.

To ensure that shared mental models can be effective , they should provide accurate and accurate information about the reality. An accurate picture is crucial when creating a realistic strategy. Without a precise view of the situation it's difficult to create an effective strategy since the initial point of departure isn't determined by the reality. A shared model of mentality must connect and align the objectives and goals of the person to the goals and visions of the organization.

Both at the personal and organizational levels, the importance of mental models that facilitate decision-making and more efficient thinking processes is not overstated. The ability to train your brain in new ways can help you to address issues that you couldn't solve previously and see opportunities that were otherwise undiscovered, and gain an objective, multi-disciplinary view of the system and world in general.

The mental model's structure is comprised of learned information and knowledge that is pre-existing or derived from previous experiences. The development of links between these facets allows the drawing of inferences from previous experiences and then these inferences can be utilized to understand the present circumstances that we are in. The experience of experiencing is one of the primary elements in the creation and evolution of models for mental processing.

Mental models are our tool to understand and explain scenarios and systems. Mental models also have predictive capabilities in their nature. They can be used to predict outcomes by using mental simulations. Through the creation of simple internal models of complicated external scenarios Mental models help us improve our understanding of complex scenarios and help us think more clearly by organizing and structuring knowledge in a way that is simple to comprehend and remember.

Mental models are invariably agents for changing behavior. They influence how we think. they eventually influence our actions as well as our behavior, and ultimately lead to the creation of habits of mind and beliefs that determine our personality. Because our behavior and actions are dependent on our knowledge of systems, when we increase our knowledge by acquiring cognitive models we are able to modify our behavior.

Mental models combine our thoughts of experiences, knowledge and experiences to build the framework that we can base our ideas. They accomplish the integration of knowledge into structured frameworks by the following steps:

The organization of background information into simple concepts

Making reference points from previous memories and experiences.

Linking facts and information.

Facilitating mental simulations that assist in the prediction of possible outcomes and to anticipate future developments.

Chapter 11: 9 Versatile Mental Models

Mental models are the frameworks which we employ to make decisions and explain what we are doing or to think about the world. They are used in our subconscious and many of them have become habitual in our daily lives. If you've ever created an unbiased list of pros and cons, considered the potential price of an event or made a decision in response to FOMO, you've used an emotional model.

We've discussed confirmation bias, a crucial one that product managers must observe, however, there are a myriad of more obscure mental models that we can employ to intentionally frame our thinking methods. When you employ mental models as a method of thinking, not simply as a reflex, they could aid in identifying paths towards better choices.

Of the thousands of mental models, some work specifically to assist teams in creating amazing products. Here's a list of nine mental models that you can apply to think about and solve issues that you have to build your product.

Mental models you need for product development:

1. Causal loops

A causal loop is method of understanding the relationships between different things by identifying positive and negative relationships. When you create causal loops you sketch out the functions of a system by describing the manner of how the various parts interact.

A simple analysis of personal productivity could be able to reveal that meditation is a good way to become more productive, however distracting themselves and engaging in hobbies can lower their efficiency:

How it will benefit to you assist you keep your eyes open by making you look at everything simultaneously. If you're focusing on a the lower than average conversion rate in the current month, or if you're beginning to see a remarkable 7-day retention and retention, causal loops may assist in identifying other variables involved in making the metrics feasible.

Thinking through causal loops can assist you in understanding the consequences of your choices prior to making them, to ensure that you aren't blinded by the results. If you choose to go the envelope for a brand new feature, you're likely to be able to see a decline in other aspect, such as fixing bugs. Knowing the connection between these two areas helps to make sure you are investing in the right way.

2. Pareto efficiency

It is the Pareto efficiency model describes an economy-based model to allocate resources, which says that you can't make a difference to one thing without compromising the other.

What it can do for you: What it does: Pareto efficiency framework offers some advantages.

It assists in balancing the need for resources and also recognizing that making something better results in a loss elsewhere other. The tool for replaying customer experiences FullStory illustrates how this can affect to customer service. When it comes to metrics for support they state "[none are "bad" They are simply blind spots that you must be aware of. ..." For instance the priority given to speed of response could bring more customers in to assist however, it comes at the expense of good quality.

For analytics, specifically the efficiency of Pareto is kept in an eye on the resource balance when deciding the solutions your data are revealing. Since it's generally easier to play around with analytics as opposed to implementing the solution, it's essential to think about what is most effective across all fields.

3. Product/market fit

Fit for market or product is a method to understand the way your product is positioned in relation to your customers. Does the market demand the product you offer? It's a fundamental mental model to build an item.

What it can do for you: Customers who are in need of or desire to purchase products are the main reason for the existence of your company. The existence of your product requires you to be aware of what your customers are doing to anticipate the needs of your customers as well possible.

That means, particularly when it comes to analytics it is essential to keep your customer in the forefront of your thoughts while making decisions. While it's tempting like you've "reached market-fit for your product" once you've got your MVP but it's possible to be a problem at any point you're trying measure the reactions of your customers, their and satisfaction.

4. Work to be done

The work to be done model can help you contemplate what you're building to aid a person in accomplishing something. The model is actually the basis of an entire blog devoted to this kind of model.

What it can do for you: This approach allows you to focus on the primary reason that users use your product. The way the product functions is much less than what people can accomplish using it. Does it meet their problems? Does it aid them in doing the job more effectively?

Particularly when it comes to analysing data, you need to be focused on what your customer is looking for and why they choose to make a decision and not only whether or not your collection of measures looks great. What are the reasons that cause users to behave as they do? How do they utilize your products features to accomplish their task? If you are analyzing your data and data, these are the kinds of questions the job to be accomplished model encourages for you to inquire.

5. Cost/Benefit Analysis

The cost-benefit model is a method of calculating the cost that weighs each decision in relation to"the "cost" (usually the fiscal cost but it can also be adjustable) in addition to the "benefit" from the suggested solution.

What can it do to help to you? Cost/benefit analyses provides more advanced form of the pros and cons especially when combined with objectives. For instance, if your main target for this month is to announce an update for your product Any additional project that slows down the release can be a cost. It can help you to focus your efforts by recognizing that the benefits of one endeavor may outweigh the expense that it will incur for the next one.

6. Pattern design

Design pattern models can be a method to reuse things that function as common solutions to everyday issues.

What can it do for you? While initially designed to be software design patterns can be utilized in any area from pipelines to analytics. You may notice that a certain group of users are significantly less active in comparison to other groups. Instead of creating a completely innovative solution, you can use a method that you had previously used in a similar scenario could be suitable for this particular group of users. Utilizing design patterns and identifying them can help you develop feasible solutions and also saves you time.

There are also anti-patterns as you begin applying design pattern-based analysis to the decision making process. Anti-patterns are a common response to issues that are detrimental. When you've established your patterns of design for any specific subject, pay attention to the outcomes you're getting from your typical "solutions" If you discover a few bad apples, take them off or find ways to improve them.

7. Reversible vs. irreversible decisions

Reversible and. irreversible model divides each choice into option of whether or not possible to be reversed. For instance purchasing a product is reverseable (ex it is possible to return it) however, firing an individual is not reversible (you cannot rescind someone's firing).

What it can do for you: When you ask yourself to make an action is reversible, and irreversible. You're clarifying the stakes of your situation. It helps you determine what decisions require greater time, effort, attention, and which can be taken quickly.

8. Pioneers as well as settlers and town planners

A pioneers', settler's and town planners models make the case that various types of thinking/talents are needed in different periods of time.

"Pioneers" bring innovation to your team and product. They're the ones who make your company or your product distinct.

"Settlers" discover ways to create an enduring product or business on the basis of what you've invented without the need to design each working component from scratch.

"Town planners" depend on models that have proved as the most effective methods of bringing something to size.

What can it do for you? This three-way breakdown of different types of hiring and kinds of ideas can help determine when it's best to come with a completely new idea or to rely on solutions already in place and cut down on time. This keeps all your resources focused in the areas which are the most profitable for them.

If you're trying figure out the areas where you've been wasting your time "innovating," try tracking your choices by categorizing them according to one of the categories above. You'll discover the areas where you could save time by implementing solutions already in place.

9. Strong viewpoint, weakly held

The strong view weakly maintained model can be a method to challenge ideas by adopting the "strong" view (one that is able to be supported) and the holder of the position "weakly" (allowing the possibility of being challenged, and looking for more information about it).

What it can do for you: Though there are occasions when an answer to a problem is clear and dry, the majority of the time what we come against isn't as simple. When data and analytics are involved It is important to establish a clear position and make a firm assertion however, it should be open to new data as it's received. This will help you reduce the influence of unconscious bias as you create clear paths and set things moving.

Important

Anyone who's stopped to consider the ways they drive now will realize that it's a lot simpler than when they first got started. In the beginning we had to be thinking about every single aspect. Regarding mirrors and turning indicators, and gauging our speed in relation the speed limit. Concerning passing traffic, oncoming the traffic and pedestrians. We wondered about how other people were judging us, whether we appeared as if we were in control , or not.

After we had completed our driving test and was driving for a few months and got into the routine. While not being aware of what we were taught in the beginning that we were taught, we quickly and subconsciously gained awareness and proficiency in driving on familiar terrain. We had, in the absence of conscious awareness, created mental models for driving in the terrain that we encountered.

Take a moment to think about your typical driving scenario. Perhaps you're located in a city and you usually travel from your home to work and back. Sounds easy enough, doesn't it? Imagine you're in vacation within the Swiss Alps. You're driving a car rental and it's dark. The weather is horrible with rain and snow coming down on the road, making it extremely slippery. In addition the fact that you missed a turning and now find yourself on a backroad which is more the goat track than a road. When you travel to the top of the hill, you see that a few rocks fall off not too far ahead of you and drop down the cliff to the goat track. What's your mood today? Focused? Alert?

We expend a lot of energy dealing with difficult and unfamiliar situations mind, it must come up with ways to make us more comfortable in the long run. It accomplishes this by simplifying many scenarios. For instance, in the first case city driving, the brain has created representations of the surroundings so that we don't need to think about the complexity of it. These representations are known by the term mental model. In the second instance goat track driving, this lack of experience indicates that the representations aren't suitable and shouldn't be used. Therefore the brain must perform and work. Consider how exhausted you feel when you get to work (first instance) as compared to when you get to the top of the hill (second).

Mental models are tiny snippets of information that are usually insufficient. However, we trust them, without ever questioning their accuracy or, in fact their accuracy. The unconscious uses of them free us from the burden of complex thinking by faking our minds. Thisis in contrast to the fact that, as Alfred Korzybski noted, "the map is not the territory"1.

Mental Models In Use

The main issue with mental models is their inability to be aware of their usage and their precision. When faced with complex situations like understanding, and making decision-making with a large amount of data from the external world, strategists often unknowingly depend on mental models. This is because mental models influence not only the way we process information, but as well the information we work with. Indeed, mental models function as filters to assist the body and the brain manage complicated information. They also help us understand the process of processing and making sense of the vast amount of data. This explains how two people who are working with the same data could come to totally different conclusions regarding it. The conclusions they draw are based on perspectives.

Conclusion

It is the next stage to begin using what you've learned in order to get the results you want quickly. There is nothing that is as effective as the mental model, and therefore having them is essential. However, it is important to be aware how mental models can be embedded within the nature of everyone. The only distinction is that some people notice that while others do not. The way you view issues or people in your life are based on what you think about as your model. The question of whether the model you have created is true or false is something you must determine and adjust in line with your findings.

With the many mental models within this publication, it is important to not be rushing through these models. Be sure to take the time to learn about each of them as they can affect you in a profound way. Your thoughts will be formed within your head, both unconsciously or consciously. You need to challenge these thoughts in order to get the most the contents of the book. Get rid of the cycle of self-loathing and self-doubt , and begin doing things that actually makes you productive.

www.ingramcontent.com/pod-product-compliance
Lightning Source LLC
Chambersburg PA
CBHW060330030426
42336CB00011B/1277